K.V. Dominic Criticism and Commentary:
Essential Readings Companion

Dr. Ramesh Chandra Mukhopadhyaya

Foreword by Dr. T.V. Reddy

From the World Voices Series

Modern History Press

Ann Arbor

K.V. Dominic Criticism and Commentary: Essential Readings Companion
Copyright © 2017 by Dr. Ramesh Chandra Mukhopadhyaya. All Rights Reserved.

Foreword by Dr. T.V. Reddy

From the World Voices Series

Library of Congress Cataloging-in-Publication Data

Names: Mukhopåadhyåaçya, Rameâsa, author.
Title: K.V. Dominic criticism and commentary : essential readings companion / Ramesh Chandra Mukhopadhyaya.
Description: Ann Arbor, MI : Modern History Press, 2017. | Series: World voices series | Includes index.
Identifiers: LCCN 2017034093 | ISBN 9781615993574 (pbk. : alk. paper)
Subjects: LCSH: Dominic, K. V. (Kannappillil Varghese), 1956---Criticism and interpretation.
Classification: LCC PR9499.4.D66 Z76 2017 | DDC 821/.92--dc23
LC record available at https://lccn.loc.gov/2017034093

Published By
Modern History Press
5145 Pontiac Trail
Ann Arbor, MI

www.ModernHistoryPress.com
info@ModernHistoryPress.com
Tollfree (USA/CAN) 888-761-6268
Elsewhere 734-417-4266

Distributed by Ingram International (USA/CAN/AU) and Bertram Books (UK/EU).

Contents

Foreword by T.V. Reddy iii

Chapter 1 - About the Poet and his Background 1
   On the Cover Page of the Book K. V. Dominic Essential Readings 2
   On the Poet and his Name... 2
   On the Poet's Native Town, Thodupuzha... 6
   Further Explanations of Sanskrit Terms 8
   Sattva, Rajah and Tamah in K. V. Dominic's works....................................... 9
   On the Poet's Home State, Kerala.. 12
   On the Poet's Country, India 16

Chapter 2 - What Led the Poet to Write Poems? 19
   On the Elegies 21
   On the Issues of Women, Parents and Old Age... 32
   The Economics of the Poet 40

Chapter 3 - Pathos in the Poems 45
   On Tragic Lives of Children 46
   On Hardships and Tears of Youth.. 48
   On Man's Selfishness and Vices 50

Chapter 4 - Criticism on Government's Claims and Promises 53
   On Family 53
   On Hunger and Poverty 55
   On Fake Development 57

Chapter 5 - Surrealism in the Poetry 59
   On Docupoetry 59
   On Violence, Terrorism and War 60
   On the Need of Harmonious Life with Nature 63

Chapter 6 - Commentary on Selected Poems 67
    Explication of the poem "Siachen Tragedy" 68
    Text and Explication of the Poem "Massacre of Cats" 70
    Explication of the Poem "Lines Composed from Thodupuzha River's Bridge" 76
    Explication of the Poem "Parental Duty" 77
    Stylistic Analysis of the Poem "Long Live E. K. Nayanar" 81

About the Author 83

Index 85

Foreword

When I received an email from Victor R. Volkman, the distinguished Editor of Modern History Press, to write a Foreword to this critical work on Dr. Dominic written by Prof. Ramesh Chandra Mukhopadhyaya, a highly distinguished and reputed scholar and critic from Kolkata, I felt extremely happy. There cannot be a greater joy for me than writing a Foreword to the standard critical work penned by my erudite friend Dr. Ramesh on the poetry of my esteemed friend Dr. Dominic who is at once a poet, critic and short story writer of equal eminence in all the aforesaid genres. My acquaintance with Dr. Dominic goes back to 2010, when I was introduced to him by our renowned friend and poet Dr. D. C. Chambial, the Editor of the illustrious literary journal *Poetcrit*. When I expressed my wish to attend the GIEWEC Literary festival that was to be organized at Ernakulam in his home State Kerala, he, being the General Secretary of the Guild of Indian English Writers Editors and Critics, courteously invited me and it gave me an opportunity to come closer to him and understand him better.

As a matter of fact, he is the main pillar of the Organization and it is no exaggeration to say that he is the active force behind it and it is on him the existence of the Guild rests. With enormous patience and tact, hard work and resourcefulness he has been organizing the Annual literary Seminars and editing two standard Journals - *Writers Editors Critics* (WEC) and *International Journal on Multicultural Literature* (IJML). I felt fortunate to find a noble friend in him and from then onwards our friendship developed with ethical and intellectual strength. Later on behalf of the members of the Guild when he proposed my name to be the Hon. President of the Guild, I happily accepted it with the sole objective of serving the cause of the Guild together with him who is the dynamic spirit behind the smooth functioning of the responsible National-level Organization.

Dr. Dominic is at once a distinguished poet, critic and short story writer. He has so far published five collections of poems in English – 1.*Winged Reason*, 2.*Write Son, Write*, 3. *Multicultural Symphony* 4. *Contemporary Concerns and Beyond* and 5. *K. V. Dominic: Essential Readings and Study Guide*. The last one has been published by Modern History Press, USA. Though he started his poetic career comparatively at a later stage, he could succeed to rise to the higher levels of poetic achievement which is indeed really great. His maiden attempt itself was a great success and from then onwards he never looked back and his poetic career has been a steady progress in technique as well as quality. Moreover, he constructs his poems on the solid foundations of everlasting ethical values and human considerations such as essential sympathetic understanding and tolerance which have transformed his poems into unfading flowers spreading the balmy breeze of their fragrance to distant lands and territories. Dr. S. Kumaran, the distinguished scholar and critic, has done a great work on Dr. Dominic by bringing out a remarkable work of critical essays, *Philosophical Musings for a Meaningful Life: An Analysis of K. V. Dominic's Poems,* published by Modern History Press, USA.

The present work by Dr. Ramesh Chandra Mukhopadhyaya, a profound scholar in English literature with equal command on the Vedic and Upanishadic knowledge which indeed forms the solid foundation of the Sanatana Dharma, which has come to be known as Hinduism, highlights the depth of Dominic's poetry, unearths the rich ores of poetic beauty hidden in the poems by his thought-provoking analytic study and enlightening interpretation of the poems in the light of Indian poetics and thought. This critical work is meant to be a Companion to Dominic's significant volume i.e. *K. V. Dominic: Essential Readings and Study Guide* with its critical analysis, interpretation, explication and elucidation of Dominic's poetry in general and the poems included in the book in particular. In this context I feel happy to say that Dr. Ramesh with his extraordinary creative and critical vision is the right person to have undertaken this critical project and he has done full justice to his work in making this critical study an in-depth work shining with gems of critical insights and groundbreaking highlights.

The great merit of this critical work, unique in its nature, is that the writer Dr. Ramesh tries to project the poetry of Dominic in the light of ancient Hindu thought which in other words is the everlasting moral path of right living which is totally free from all these narrow barriers and dogmas and which rests only on kindness and compassion to all living creatures. The greatness of the poet Dr. Dominic is that, though he is a Christian by birth, he never allows himself to be bound by any religious dogma and his poetry proves him to be a true son of the Indian soil known from times immemorial for the catholicity of outlook and compassion to fellow beings irrespective of their caste, creed and faith. And what is commendable in the poet Dr. Dominic is the indisputable fact that the essential spirit of The Hindu thought flows in his blood and genes which got internalized in his psyche. Likewise, the eminence of the critic Dr. Ramesh Chandra Mukhopadhyaya lies in the fact that he has succeeded in the critical task of his superb explication of the poems in unravelling this inner vision underlined in the poems, in focussing on the human values embedded in the poems and in giving philosophical treatment to the poems of Dr. Dominic in the background of this Sanatana Dharma on which India rests. It is difficult to find another critic of the stature of Dr. Ramesh in the critical explanation of the poem in the light of Indian poetics that has come down to us from more than two thousand years.

About the Poet and his Background

This critical work is divided into six chapters. While the first chapter deals with the poet and his background, the second explains what led the poet to write poems and the third and the fourth attempt to bring out the pathos in the poems and the reality of the fate of Government's claims and promises respectively. The fifth chapter is on "Surrealism in the Poetry" and speaks on violence, terrorism and war and on the need of harmonious life with nature, while the last one is a commentary on selected poems ending with a fitting conclusion.

Dr. Ramesh begins this critical work with the aesthetic explication of the picture on the cover of the book displaying two children together, one white and the other black; this metaphorical presentation takes him back to Blake's poem 'The Little Black Boy' which in turn suggests the metaphorical nature of the poems in the book i.e. the truth lies neither in the white nor in the black, but somewhere else as it is elusive. As a matter of fact, the search for truth, the endless search for the Absolute Truth, should be the sole aim of the human being here on this earth. Even a casual glance at the front cover of the book rouses the curiosity of the reader and kindles the inquisitive mind to go straight into the pages to taste the fruits of the contents of the poems.

The poem 'Onam' (p.37) by Dominic is a description of the most popular festival in his home State of Kerala celebrated as a State Festival in August-September. It is a harvest festival celebrated all over the State by all the people irrespective of religion, caste or creed and Keralites staying in different parts of the country and in foreign shores come to their native place to participate in this most important festival. This festival is in the memory of their ancient mighty King Maha Bali who ruled all the three worlds without any opposition. It is celebrated for ten days and each day is a wonder of new robes, sweets and feasts ringing with Onam songs, plays and dances and giving the feel of the age-old culture and tradition of the people of Kerala. Onam songs in praise of Mahabali are sung through generations inspiring younger minds with the spirit of courage and sacrifice:

> the golden rule of Maveli
> ....
> Equality prevailed in the society;
> no lies, no crimes, no deceits;
> and no cheat; no poverty, no child death.
> All were happy.   (*K. V. Dominic: Essential Readings*, pp.37-38)

Boat race is the star attraction of this festival in this sea coast State known for its backwaters of the Arabian Sea and criss-crossing rivers and streams. Boat race or *vallam kali* takes place among snake-shaped boats with more than a hundred energetic youth rhythmically rowing with oars and singing at the same time with gusto.

This critical treatise as a matter of fact commences with the interpretation of the poem 'What is Karma?' (*K.V. Dominic: Essential Readings*, p.248) where Dominic makes use of the concept of Karma, one of the cardinal tenets of the Hindu philosophy, the other concepts being Atma, Maya and Samskara. Here the critic Dr. Ramesh is at his best in exploring the meaning to its depth and explaining in detail the background for a fuller understanding of the concept of Karma by the reading community outside India. The nature of Karma is decided by the degree of the presence of the three qualities—Sattwa, Rajas and Tamas and by the legacy of the inherited Samskaras. Dr. Ramesh is full of appreciation to the dialogue form observed by the poet and he rightly says "This reminds us of Plato's *Dialogues* and *Ramakrishna Kathamrita*" and adds that "The Indian approach to things is qualitative or founded on guna or quality."(p.7). Now while explaining the poem 'Lines Composed from Thodupuzha River's Bridge' the critic says it "reminds us of the lines 'Composed upon Westminster Bridge' by Wordsworth and invites comparison" with Wordsworth's poem written in the year 1802. First let us have a look at the lines of Dominic:

> Looking down from your girdle bridge
> my eyes and my mind bathe in thy morning beauty.
> (*K. V. Dominic: Essential Readings*, p.138)

Now look at the lines of Wordsworth:

> Earth has not anything to show more fair
> Dull would be he of soul who could pass by.

Dr. Ramesh makes a comparative study: "While Wordsworth marvels at the sight of the majestic morning of London, Dominic bathes in the river of life and light and we too bathe with him and feel the touch of the flowing nectar."(p.10). In another context, Ramesh says "The poet Dominic is so much in love with his native land that he cannot migrate from here despite the fact that it is being turned into a wasteland"(p.15).

Dominic's lines on Mother India, 'Victory to thee Mother India' (p.92) bristles with the patriotic spirit of the poet:

> Victory to thee Mother India;
> for you did unite the races
> divided on religion,
> culture, language and colour.
> . . . .
> A hundred years back
> thy great son, Tagore
> sang in praise of you.
> Matha, you could rouse then
> the hearts of Punjab, Sind, Gujarat,
> Maratha, Dravida, Orissa and Bengal.

In the words of Dr. Ramesh "This poem not only echoes the national song but also speaks of the deep influence that Tagore cast upon Dominic".

Now the critic comes to the beginning of the poetic career of Dr. Dominic, which is quite a significant event that lasts long in our memory. He composed his first poem when he was 48 years old and he describes the situation in his Preface to his *Essential Readings* thus:

> "One of my colleagues Prof. George Joson of the Dept. of Mathematics drowned in a river as he was driving back to his house at 11 p.m. on 14 May 2004. It was raining cats and dogs throughout the night and the body was found out in the early morning frozen in the driver's seat of his car... Joson was my intimate friend, living with his unemployed wife and three little daughters, resembling three angels, just two hundred metres away from my house. Thus my 'bad heart' heavy and brimming with grief released the tension on paper after two days."

Dr. Ramesh appropriately compares this situation to the more moving situation of the great ancient Indian poet Valmiki whose grief came out in the form a *sloka* when he saw the male crowncha bird killed with the hunter's arrow when it was in love play with its female partner. Thus Valmiki became the first poet in the world literature with his immortal Sanskrit epic *The Ramayana*. The lines of Dominic's poem 'In Memoriam George Joson' (*K. V. Dominic: Essential Readings*, p.1) move the heart of the reader and penetrate into deeper truths of life:

> The most painful was the sight
> when your youngest kid,
> not knowing what has happened,
> kissed your face often
> and plucked flowers
> from your wreath;
> tossed them to her sisters weeping and screaming.

Dr. Dominic's poem 'An Elegy on My Ma' (p.91) is an expression of his unbounded love for his departed mother and a description of her suffering for six long years before death. He recollects—'Your sleepless nights, / sitting and wheezing, / when we were fast asleep, / . . . / Long six years, / bewailing often / "Why doesn't God, / call me back?'.The stark truth of honesty as well as the apprehensiveness of the uncertainty of the personal security in the last days finds a faithful expression in the poem: 'Ma, you were never / deserted by your children. / What would be our Fate, ma, / when we become old as you?' Here Dr. Ramesh says with an air of critical humour: 'We have caught Dominic off his guard. Firstly it is here that Dominic gives vent to real anxieties."

Cruelty prevailing in general in the world and particularly in families and schools is described in poems such as 'Rahul's World', 'Nature Weeps' etc. Harmony in the domestic life gets ruined when the drunken husband comes home and beats his wife and son. The poet conjures up the scene so realistically that it lingers long before our mind's screen: 'Drunken father / beat mother, / beat Rahul;

/ Kicked away supper, / None could sleep. / Cruel father, / Cruel teacher, / Cruel world, / Poor Rahul / longs for love'. (p.39).The other poem presents the cruelty of the teacher towards the students in the school which is the main reason for most of the dropouts in the schools: 'The child is reluctant / to go to school: / teacher welcomes with cane' (p.117).

In Chapter 4 the critic deals with the poets' criticism on Government's liberal promises which are conveniently forgotten immediately after the elections and on claims which are blatant lies. Refuting the claims of the Government that India is on the way to become number one in the world, the poet brings out the shocking reality in the poems 'India Number One (p.166) and 'Rocketing Growth of India!'(p.121):

> Ninety-seven percent of my countrymen
> have no access to clean drinking water.
> Yet the Government claims
> the country is fast growing!
> True, growth is there in numbers of multi-millionaires
> who are even less than two-percent, (p.166)

The highlight of the Chapter 5 is the critical reflection of the poem 'To My Colleague' (p.126) which presents the most moving word-painting on the ruthless cruelty of the communal fanatics who are worse than barbarians, indeed an indelible blot on the civilized humanity as a whole. The right palm of the Professor TJ in a college in Kerala was hacked off by inhuman members of a viciously fanatic community, ordered by their fanatic court, for speaking on a secular point. They further axed his left leg from thigh to toes and cut three fingers and bones of his left palm. The right palm was picked up by his sister and it was stitched in the hospital 'as a dry branch budded to a live plant'. The climax reaches when he is suspended and dismissed by the college he has served with utmost sincerity and sacrifice. The critic Dr. Ramesh is at his best in interpreting this ghastly situation:

> "It is more fearsome than Banquo's ghost. Neither Kyd nor Seneca could portray such figures. Facts are stranger than fiction. The image of TJ maimed and mutilated reminds of the aesthetics of cruelty as propounded by Antonin Artaud."

Chapter 6 deals with the writer's commentary on selected poems and begins with the explication of the poem 'Siachen Tragedy' which is a vivid description of the snow-clad Siachen glacier in the Himalayas and a moving narration of the natural calamity resulting in the death of many soldiers as well as civilians who got buried by the fury of the avalanche. Army camps are stationed at the Siachen heights and it is the highest battle ground in the world where Indian and Pakistan soldiers have to fight with freezing temperature. Now Dr. Ramesh gives his analytical interpretation of the poem 'Massacre of Cats', comparatively a longer poem running into 83 lines. It is at once an elegy on the death of seven cats poisoned by a neighbour, a commentary on the cruelty of the human beings and a plea for compassion to all living creatures:

> Birds and animals play
> their assonant keys.
> Man alone strikes discordant notes. (*ER*, p.76)

Thus this critical work *K. V. Dominic Criticism and Commentary: Essential Readings Companion* by Dr. Ramesh Chandra Mukhopadhyaya is not only an extremely well-written critical document with Indian insights into the poetry of Dominic, but a great contribution to the corpus of literary criticism with its prime focus on Indian aesthetics and psyche. With his extensive scholarship both in Indian and European classics and modern writings he has accomplished this rare work of explicating the numerous nuances in the poetry of Dr. Dominic and interpreting the poems altogether from a new critical perspective based on Indian poetics.

Note: Textual quotations are from the book *K. V. Dominic Essential Readings and Study Guide*.

by Prof. T.V. Reddy (Poet, Critic &Novelist)

Chapter 1 - About the Poet and his Background

It is said that the *history* plays of Shakespeare help one to better understand the history of England than volumes on British History. And it is better to read the poems composed by K. V. Dominic to understand India of our times than perusing volumes on Indian economics, Indian politics and Indian society of today. This is not all. Poetry is at bottom a criticism of life. If this be true, then Dominic has no peer in the context of Indian English literature. In order that searching criticism could be done, there must be a high moral standard in the light of which the criticism would be possible. Dominic's poetry, unlike much of our poetry today, speaks of high moral values that are at the core Indian and that could be emulated by other cultures also. Moral values, in order to be practicable, need a grasp on the economic, political and social condition of the society under study. It also needs a comprehensive grasp on the philosophy, on the background of which the socially aware poetry could be composed.

Though Dominic's poems are not philosophical on the surface, it seems that Dominic has a philosophical system of his own which is unique and very much Indian. If anyone starts reading his poetry, he cannot stop. Dominic is irresistible because of his simplicity of parole below which lurks a deeply visionary message. Here is a humble attempt to decode his poems. The text is not there in the printed material. The text is in the minds of the readers. There are as many texts as there are readers of a particular book of poems. I must acknowledge that I am not a seer who can unravel universal truths. Hence the present write-up is composed often in the first person. When you find good poetry you cannot but share your feelings with your fellow readers. Hence this book! If it provokes a few readers to read Dominic more and to plunge in what Dominic calls sattvika karma, the present reader will be more than obliged to his readers. With deepest regards to all,

Dr. Ramesh Chandra Mukhopadhayay

On the Cover Page of the Book K. V. Dominic Essential Readings

A paratext is the threshold of a text. It includes the cover along with illustration with it if any, the name of the author, the name of the editor if any. It is the link between the text and off text. Its importance cannot be exaggerated. Once upon a time, a drama with deeper message was advertised as one that bursts with laughter. When the spectators entered the theatre hall, their expectations were belied. They left the hall in the midst of the play. The advertisement was the paratext. But the drama, which is a comedy or a play, pleasant and unpleasant in the course of time, found a niche in the realm of literature. At the moment, we have a book with the names—*K. V. Dominic Essential Readings and Study Guide*. The name K. V. Dominic is kept separate from the rest. Often the name of an author stands for the works by the author. This is an instance of metonymy. There is an illustration on the cover above the names. There are two children together there--one is whitish and another black. Is it a metaphor–a comparison between two apparently unlike things? It at once reminds us of William Blake:

> My mother bore me in the southern wild,
> And I am black, but O! my soul is white;
> White as an angel is the English child:
> But I am black as if bereav'd of light.
>
> (Blake, "The Little Black Boy")

The illustration brings a black child and a white child together and announces aloud that neither black is the truth nor white is the truth. Neither not black is the truth nor not white is the truth. Truth is elsewhere perhaps. Thus the cover page of the book evokes expectations in the readers that they will come across some emergent truths in the text if they ever take the pains to go through the same.

On the Poet and his Name

The paratext informs us that the book contains poems. In fact genres are *sine qua non* not only in our everyday world, but also in the field of art. Does anyone go for prayer in a post office? Does anyone go to post a letter at a church? Similarly if any one infers from the paratext of a book that it should be a horror story, and if to his/her utter dismay the text is found to be a tale of love, will s/he not be disappointed? Since the *Essential Readings and Study Guide* is a book of poems about social justice, women's rights and the environment, the mindset of the readers are prepared for such poetryscapes.

But before that the readers are ordinarily apt to question--who is the poet? The answer is K. V. Dominic. In other words K. V. Dominic is the efficient cause and words are material cause. Whenever an event takes place, especially in the realm of human relationship we ask who has been the cause or architect of the event. Well as Hume observes there is no necessary connection between a cause and effect. Kant tells us that cause is not there in the world. Cause is a priori form of intuition which we add to the world. Even if we agree with the notion of causality we feel that there cannot be a single cause behind any effect or a poem for our purpose. K. V. Dominic could not write these poems if there were no social injustices. Had he been born during the rule of Mahabali or Maveli he would have no occasion to write such poems. Because during Maveli's golden rule:

> Equality prevailed in the society;
> no lies, no crimes, no deceits;
> and no cheat;
> no poverty, no child death.
> All were happy;
> heaven cannot be different! ("Onam" 38)

In short no one cause, in other words, Dominic has not been alone responsible for the poems that he has written. Countless causes and condition have been responsible for composing the poems. Dominic has been simply instrumental in this poetic activity. The groans of the society today seem to have snatched the pen of Dominic to write in their bare sheer wailing and thundering style. But read the poems. Why ask who wrote it? Discussing the life and times of the author shifts the spotlight from the text to extra-textual things. Roland Barthes has already announced the death of an author. There is no organic relationship between the signifier and the signified. Every language has its own syntax idioms and way of manifesting itself. When the poet seeks to express himself through a language he must obey the rules of the language and thereby he is carried away from his objective. Besides, language springs in response to language spoken earlier. Hence no poet can express himself through language. So no poet writes a poem. Despite that we cling to the myth that a piece of poetry is composed by a person called poet.

Barthes points out that the origin of a work may be with the author but the destination of the work lies with the reader. The work may have been a three dimensional one forged by the author. But when it is photographed by the readers' mind it becomes two dimensional. The reader adds a third dimension to the work from his mental and spiritual resources. So where is the text? It is half created and half perceived. The text is in the readers' mind. Hence the author dies and the reader is born while decoding a text. And the present portrayal of Dominic's poetry partially owes to the understanding of the poems by the present reader. This must be acknowledged. We cannot study anything objectively or as it is. If we want to determine the speed of an electron we cannot determine its speed and vice versa.

Close reading method does not take any extra-textual account of the poet. With close reading school, who is the poet? S/he who has written the poem? What is the poem? What the poet has written is the poem? It is something like–Whose house is this? This is Ram's house. Who is Ram? Ram is the person who lives in this house. This is argument along a vicious circle. We propose to read the poems of Dominic from Close Reading point of view.

Close reading school reads the text and not the extra-textual context in the background of the same. In that case we might ask what the name Dominic means. Dominic is a Roman Catholic name which means 'Of Our Lord'. Curiously enough we have also a Dominique in Sefirah. Dominique is another version of Dominic. Our Dominique de Miscault who is a great artist in her own right is also God's own. Spiritualism in art is what constitutes her aesthetics. She is an abstract artist. One wonders whether spiritualism lurks in the poetry of K. V. Dominic also who is under our study.

Well the book of poems by Dominic under study has a poem entitled "Who am I? Does not the name of the poem remind the reader of the great philosopher Sankaracharya who cried: Who are you? Who am I? Where from have we come? Who is my mother? Who is my father? Once someone seeks to probe into the essence of the other, one is apt to probe into the essence if any of himself/herself.

And let us see how Dominic describes himself:

> "Who are you?" my superego asked
> "I am Prof. K. V. Dominic, MA, M.Phil, PhD," my id replied
> "Alright, what else?"
> "English poet, short story writer, critic, editor."
> "Keep that long tail under your armpit," superego exploded.
> "An illiterate farmer is greater than you;
> His service is greater than your scribbling; ("Who am I?" 196)

We have asked who Dominic is. And Dominic himself has taken a pre-emptive step. He has written the poem "Who am I?" Whenever a person asks himself/herself "Who am I?" s/he is divided between the observer and the observed of his/her own self. In other words, Where is Dominic? There is the observer Dominic and the observed Dominic. Dominic borrows terms from Freudian psychology and thereby he is not one but three in superego, ego and id. In Vedanta there is the self which is made of food. In that shell there is the life force as self. Inside that there is the self as mind. Below that there is the self made of knowledge. Below that there is the self that is all bliss. Thus where is Dominic, Dominic is not found. If a person is not one, but six persons, the person is not there.

Every work of poetry has the open sesame hidden in it to guide the readers how to decode it. And may be Dominic's poetry demands psychological approach to his poems. The interior dialogue between the superego and the id makes the poem "Who am I?" a curious literary type and teaches us to probe into our own selves. Where is the self?--one is apt to ask.

Well, let us go back to our question, *Who is Dominic?* Perhaps we can approach this with a related question: Who was his mother? Who was his father?

"An Elegy on My Ma" gives us a vivid pen-picture of Dominic's mother and Dominic's childhood and Dominic's attitude to his mother tongue or Indian vernaculars. When he writes about his mother he does not use the word mother in the title of his poem. Mother is substituted by the Indian ma. Because one whose mother tongue teaches one to call his mother as ma cannot address his dear mother in a foreign tongue. This shows that Dominic is an Indo-English poet. And what does Dominic tell about his ma?

> Ma, I do remember
> the brambly path
> you treaded for decades;
> How you raised
> your brothers and sisters
> when your parents died;
> Struggled hard for sustenance
> even after marriage;
> How much you suffered
> bearing six sons
> in your womb!
> Ma, how can I forget
> the way you reared us?
> Dawn to dusk
> worked on the farm;
> Made the field fertile
> with gallons of sweat.
> We were never starved,
> nor knew any poverty.
>
> ("An Elegy on My Ma" 89)

A wonderful poem! In the patriarchal society we cannot talk much about our mother. We do talk about our father. But here Dominic has to tell many things about his mother. From the very childhood Dominic's mother had to face adversity. Early in her life she lost her father. She did not lie low in the face of adversity. She raised her brothers when she was a virgin. After marriage she bore six children. She worked hard in the farm. And mark you, she did not let her children starve and feel the pangs of poverty. This description of the mother teaches us how mothers can live two hundred percent, hundred percent working outdoor and hundred percent working in the household. In countryside even today mothers do work at par with the fathers. There is no gender discrimination. Gender discrimination came upon the scene with the advent of capitalism and western culture. Capitalism selected the males for technical education and the women were cast into the household. Landed property was registered in the name of the male *karta* of a Hindu Undivided Family (HUF). The poem does show what great potential the women have to build the nation.

An HUF is a legal term related to the Hindu Marriage Act. The female members are also given the right of share to the property in the HUF. The term finds reference in the provisions of the Income Tax Act, but the expression is not defined in the act.

The Hindu Joint family is headed by a *karta*, meaning manager, who is usually the oldest male person, who makes decisions on economic and social matters on behalf of the entire family. The patriarch's wife generally exerts control over the household and minor religious practices and often wields considerable influence in domestic matters. Family income flows into a common pool, from which resources are drawn to meet the needs of all members, which are regulated by the heads of the family

Perhaps the physiocrats are the economists in the right sense of the term. Quesney the father of physiocratic economics observed farming as the chief economic activity. The farmers need houses to live in and clothes to wear. These minor activities are assigned to artisans and industry. If the income from agriculture and the same from cricket are added the GDP might look formidable. But if food is not there what gain is there in the income from cricket? Two horses and two economists are two horses and two economists. They are not four. There must be weighting given to the source of income. Income from agriculture and income from industry are not at par.

And surely farming here might be used as a metaphor. The whole country lies fallow. We need mothers who must work at the fields and make the soil fertile.

Dominic, a master of irony in verbal communication, does not utter a single word against women having many children. He is a common man like us addressing the common folk. In fact, true human emotions breathe through his poems. Richly wrought thoughts and sentiments of the elite and the learned do not suffocate the language of his poems. "An Elegy on My Ma" by Dominic shows that Dominic's parents were farmers. When Dominic says that his mother did not let him and his brothers feel the chill of penury, we infer that he was not born with silver spoon. He was rather born in a poor family. And when we learn that he is an M A, M Phil, Ph D, it is anybody's guess how great Dominic had to suffer to climb the so called higher echelon of the society. But Dominic is not at all proud because of that. He frankly tells us that an illiterate farmer is better than us, the professors and officers and industrialists. We need rice and wheat and barley. If the farmers all over the globe go on strike for a week, are the legislators in the American Senate any good? President Trump needs two square meals a day. Or else how can he come to the White House in time. Ours is a civilization where the expenditure on overhead exceeds what we really produce. Ha Hah!

On the Poet's Native Town, Thodupuzha

Now, the present reader is curious to know in which town or village or city Dominic lives. Dear fellow readers, do not be cross with me. Curiosity is the lifeblood of human civilization. Or else why should we bother to know which dramas were composed by Shakespeare? Do chimpanzees or lions have such curiosity? That is why they have no culture and no civilization. Aristotle wrote physics and dwelled on metaphysics. While physics is concerned with the world of senses, metaphysics is concerned with the beyond. Man is never content with the contingent. He is always eager to lift up the veil that surrounds the existence to know the whole truth about the existence. Disinterested curiosity is also the life blood of science. In this context, the present author would most humbly request his fellowmen not to look down upon the neighbours who are fond of washing the dirty linen in public. They are the unacknowledged poets, critics, scientists and so on. Were they absent from the society there would be no human civilization.

Sorry for the digression. Our question at the outset was about the whereabouts of Dominic. Where does he live? Our close reading school does not let us ponder over any extra-textual context. But Dominic's poetry is imbued with much of *sattvika guna*.

Guṇa (Sanskrit) depending on the context means 'string, thread or strand', or 'virtue, merit, excellence', or 'quality, peculiarity, attribute, property'. There are three guṇas called: sattva (goodness, constructive, harmonious), rajas (passion, active, confused), and tamas (darkness, destructive, chaotic).

Well the guṇas are cornerstone of Hindu philosophy and Dominic a Christian though has assimilated Hindu philosophy. He is not a Hindu, but he is an Indian and his being is a melting pot of everything whatever excellent in Indian thought. Christianity is also an Indian religion. While the Anglo Saxons were Christianised in the 6th century, we Indians became Christians only in the 1st century AD. It was Saint Thomas who taught us Christianity.

Dominic uses the paradigm of guna in the poem "What is Karma?"

> "...................
> Three types of karmas:
> Tamasik, Rajasik, Satvik."
> "Kindly explain, Father."
> "Speech and deeds not caring result,
> minding not feelings and emotions,
> just like the action of a terrorist
> is Tamasik, which you shall never do.
> Words and actions
> done to please oneself
> fall under selfish Rajasik karma.

("What is Karma?" 248)

The first thing that strikes the reader is that it is a Christian Father or priest who speaks of Indian philosophy. Indian Christian Fathers are no less Indian than any Hindu Indian. The poem is in the dialogue form. This reminds us of Plato's *Dialogues* and *Ramkrisna Kathamrita*. The dialogue form is very apt for teaching thoughts that the world does not pay heed to.

Here we had better dwell on the guna approach to karma. The approach of so called science is quantitative and not qualitative. Science can describe how hydrogen and oxygen mingle to make water. But science cannot tell us how the emergent qualities like waterness of water, its liquidity, its thirst quenching power are derived from hydrogenness of hydrogen and oxygenness of oxygen. As long as the approach of science remains quantitative no viable philosophy of life can be raised on the foundation of science. The Indian approach to things is qualitative or founded on guna or quality. Science can describe what constitutes sugar. But if there is no sugarness in the sugar will it be sugar?

The Indian approach posits that three qualities are inherent in all things. They are *sattva, rajah and tamah*. These three Sanskrit terms are detailed in the poem "What is Karma" (Essential Readings 248-249)

- Speech and deeds that do not care for the result and not minding feelings and emotions, just like the action of a terrorist, is Tamasik.
- Words and actions done to please oneself fall under selfish Rajasik karma.
- Words and deeds done to serve others are selfless Satvik karma.

Every person has all these three gunas or qualities of which one will be dominant over the other two and that determines his/her nature. People having sattva guna as dominant or satvik people are very few in this world.

Further Explanations of Sanskrit Terms

The three gunas—sattva, raja, and tama result in five states of the mind, and every person has a distinct personality because of this. The first is Moorhavastha in which tama guna dominates and sattva and raja remain dormant. This state is triggered by passion, anger, lust, greed and possessiveness. A person could, therefore, be inclined towards sin, ignorance, nihilism and desire. This state of mind also gives rise to meanness.

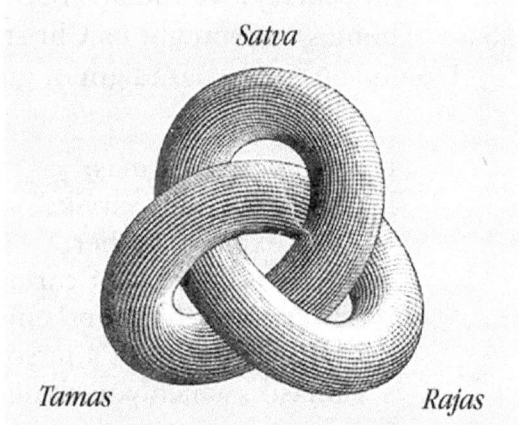

The second is Khshiptavasthaa in which raja guna is dominant and the other two are dormant. This state is brought about by feelings of love or hatred. A person in Khshiptavasthaa is often inclined or attracted towards contradictory forces like religion or sin, love or hate, attachment or renunciation, knowledge or ignorance. Thus, when sattva guna overpowers raja guna, the mind tilts towards religion, love, attachment and knowledge; when raja guna overpowers sattva guna, the opposite happens.

The third is Vikshiptavastha, in which sattva guna dominates over raja and tama gunas. Vikshiptavastha is attained by abandoning feelings of love and hate, passion and anger, greed and possessiveness and by working without desire. In this state, a person is inclined towards religion, knowledge, affluence and asceticism, but he could also go insane due to the presence of raja guna. Intellectual and inquisitive people usually go into this state of mind. But in spite of being an elevated state, this is not a normal condition because the mind is influenced by external factors.

The fourth is Ekagravastha in which thought is focused on a single subject. This is a natural state, in which the mind is not influenced by external factors. In this state, the mind becomes completely pure. This is achieved by constant practice of dhyaan or meditation. In yoga, this state is called Sampragyat Samadhi. The practitioner interacts with forces of nature, becomes discerning and appreciates the difference between mind and atmaan.

The fifth is Niruddhavastha. A practitioner achieves this state after Ekagravastha with rigorous practice. After reaching this stage, he develops a special kind of asceticism referred to as a satiric trait or condition of the mind. The practitioner gets attached to this trait and either negates or restricts the possibilities of asceticism. Thus, after negating or controlling all hindrances, he reaches the stage of Niruddhavastha where all acquired and communicated sanskaaras are destroyed.

Sattva, Rajah and Tamah in K. V. Dominic's works

In any *thing* whatever, these three qualities must exist together. Even in a poem. But in some things sattva is dominant. In some things rajah is dominant. In some other things tamah is dominant. Thus things become respectively sattvika, rajasika, and tamasika. Dominic has dwelled on these three gunas in relation to karma with wonderful precision seldom found in textbooks of Indian philosophy. Whatever activity is not tamasika and rajasika is sattvika. Well writing poetry is also a karma. It is often a social act by a lonely man. With the present reader Dominic's poetry is sattvika in essence. Because its spirit is altruistic. One of the qualities of sattva is that it is open and above board it illuminates everything. It is light unlike tamas which is heavy and which has affinity to darkness. Now since sattvaguna is predominant in Dominic's poetry it is not difficult to find out where he lives. Yes, let us read "Lines Composed from Thodupuzha River's Bridge."

The very name "Lines Composed from Thodupuzha River's Bridge" reminds us of the lines "Composed upon Westminster Bridge" by William Wordsworth. Wordsworth's poem opens with:

> Earth has not anything to show more fair:
> Dull would he be of soul who could pass by
> ("Composed upon Westminster Bridge, September 3, 1802")

In Wordsworth the poet posits that those who ignore the beauty of the scenery at Westminster Bridge while passing by are dull of soul. Wordsworth does not address the bridge endearingly. There is no evidence of his kinship with London. But Dominic's "Lines Composed from Thodupuzha River's Bridge" opens with:

> Looking down from your girdle bridge
> my eyes and my mind bathe in thy morning beauty.
> ("Lines Composed from Thodupuzha River's Bridge" 138)

Here Thodupuzha, and not the readers is the addressee. The poet endearingly observes that the bridge is the girdle of Thodupuzha. Thus it seems that there is some sort of kinship of the poet with Thodupuzha. And if we guess that Dominic is the resident of Thodupuzha it will not be far away from truth. Because in the whole poetical work there is no other name of a village or of a town addressed endearingly.

Thodupuzha is an ancient town in Kerala 200 kilometres away from Trivandrum, the State capital. There are Jain and Buddhist relics in the neighbourhood dating back to 300 BC. But it is the town that touches the river or 'puzha.' And it is the place where a rivulet or 'thodu' has become a river or 'puzha.' In other words Thodupuzha is a town caressed by a river and it is the privileged place where there has been a phase shift in the course of a river. The river is as it were inalienable from the town and the town itself is surely a river changing ceaselessly since time immemorial.

The very title of the poem "Lines Composed from Thodupuzha River's Bridge" invites comparison with Wordsworth's "Composed upon Westminster Bridge." While Wordsworth's poem is a regular sonnet with three quatrains and a clinching couplet Dominic's poem consists of fifteen lines. But Dominic's poem is also sonnet-like in its reticence. Wordsworth finds London donning the morning which will be doffed presently. London clothed in morning is majestic in its calm only because of the mighty heart lying still along with houses and ships and domes and temples open to the fields and the skies. But after an hour and so the mighty heart will be awake and smoke will cover the sky and rob the Sun of its brightness. Thus time is also a motif in the poem. The calm of the morning is destined to be shattered by the noon time city life. Dominic's poem is a companion one to Wordsworth's. True that "Every second passed in our lives / is irredeemably lost forever. / . . . / The waters that I gaze now also flow beyond my eyes. ("Lines Composed from Thodupuzha River's Bridge" 138) But this is true in the contingent. The river Thodupuzha however represents time in fast motion--Time flashes in a meteoric speed and hence we cannot brood over every second of time flowing by. The river stands for the flow of time. It springs from Sahyadri to pour down into infinite ocean.

Geologically speaking, Sahyadri harks back to the time when Gondwana broke apart. Legends tell us that Parasurama the incarnation of Vishnu hurled his axe into the seas which reached Kanyakumari. The larger part of South India was at that time occupied by the sea. The sea out of its bounty gave away the whole tract of land to the sage and withdrew the waves from there. Sahyadri has been depicted as the abode of gods. In other words Sahyadri is timeless. The river Thodupuzha springs from the timeless hills only to meet the timeless seas. In other words human life moves from one eternity to another eternity and hence although in the contingent everything is transitory like the morning descried in London, in the seer eyes of Dominic every moment is eternal and every moment is sacred. While Wordsworth marvels at the sight of the majestic morning of London, Dominic bathes in the river of life and light and we too bathe with him and feel the touch of the flowing nectar. Thus while Wordsworth's poem is gloomy, scared of the mighty heart waking up in no time, Dominic's poem is charged with an everlasting yes telling us that whether awake or asleep we are bathing in the stream of nectar. While Wordsworth's poem dwells on a transitory moment the poem of Dominic transports us from the transitory to the eternal. Any drop that comes from the eternal and merges with the eternal is eternal. This we can assert without any misgiving.

Parks in India are as old as civilization. The Ramayana describes Ayodhya as littered with parks and fountains. But most of the parks nowadays in India are perhaps forged on the model of parks in England, first envisioned by Ebenzer Howard. In order to do away the alienation of urban people from Nature, Ebenzer first introduced town planning decked with parks. The Municipal Park in Thodupuzha has figured in the works of Dominic.

Thodupuzha Municipal Park beckons the poet in the evening to unburden the cares of a life getting and spending—a haven for townsmen fleeing from the burning houses. The burning houses might remind one of Bunyan. Bunyan's hero found the city he inhabited burning. And he asked everyone to leave the city in quest of peace. And Dominic feels that every house in modern urban life is in flames. Hence people come to parks in the neighbourhood of Nature to get some respite.

Dominic gives a beautiful pen-picture of Thodupuzha park:

> Though not vast, an ideal park
> Full of trees and river adjacent
> Symphony of the chirpings from above
> Rustling of gentle breeze on leaves
> Mixed sounds of flowing vehicles
>
> ("Thodupuzha Municipal Park" 202)

This could be an archetype of Eden. But in this Eden the sound of flowing vehicles and the rustling of trees mingle. With Dominic perhaps civilization must be two hundred percent--hundred percent urban and hundred percent sylvan. In this confluence of the urban and sylvan in the park the sight of the little children playing reminds Dominic of his childhood days. Once he was swinging from a rope and he fell there from. His dear mother beat him in consequence instead of saying sympathetic words to him. That childhood of the poet is no more.

A score year back the poet visited the park with his two kids and they enjoyed the park with great joy. But alas! Those children are grown up and away. They are no more with the poet. Thus the poet describes his predicament at an age when he cannot go back to his childhood and when his own children are grown up. Nowadays nuclear families alone survive in the towns. And when children are away the parents suffer from a kind of alienation. This is a commonplace mental state of parents who have presently crossed the middle age of life. Dominic excels in depicting the mental state of common place situations. He is not after themes earmarked for poetry. Anything could be a theme of his poems.

The present poem not only dwells on an aspect of Thodupuzha his hometown, but also describes the predicament of his mind set at a particular age where is heard the mingled measure of the fountain and the cave, and how he passes his days at Thodupuzha. The high brow among the readers might debunk the poem as on too commonplace a theme. But many of us the readers at the age of fifty or sixty will find our heartfelt feelings described in the poem with telling power.

On the Poet's Home State, Kerala

There is a tribe of intellectuals who are internationalists before they are nationalists. They can go against the interests of their nation to serve some foreign power whom they worship. But this is not natural. Every man loves himself. At the same time he loves his mother. That is why we love ourselves and love our family. We love our family and at the same time we love our town. We love our town and we love our State. Thodupuzha is in Kerala. And the poet's love for his State is time and again.

In the elegy written on the death of E. K. Nayanar, Dominic exclaims:

> It is impossible to believe
> our dearest CM is no more.
>
> ("Long Live E. K. Nayanar" 3)

E. K. Nayanar belonged to Kerala. And he was three times the CM of Dominic's State Kerala. Nayanar's demise came upon the poet as a great shock. Because Nayanar was an epitome of ideal leader of the people. His heart was full of the milk of love and compassion which are essence of socialism according to Dominic. And surely though a communist and though he was accused of being pro China during Chinese aggression, with Dominic Nayanar was truly a patriot. He had no foes, only friends. He championed the cause of the denied and the deprived. Dominic calls Nayanar a rare species of a communist. True. Because communists have unlike Nayanar class enemies. Unlike Nayanar, the communists are internationalists first obeying Comintern and then patriots.

Dominic describes the Onam vividly. It is a harvest festival taking place in the month of Chingam–either in August or in September. People of Kerala must come home during the festival even from far countries. Children run for flowers in the morning and make 'pookalams' in the courtyard or at the entrance of their house. 'Poo' means flowers and 'kalam' means arrangement. In the language of the poet:

> Pookalams with

myriads of flowers
in circular pattern:
a fantastic sight!

("Onam" 37)

This floral design on the floor is forged to welcome Mahabali, once upon a time the king of the three worlds. Onam is a festival that continues for ten days. Each day a fresh circle is forged. On the first day there is one circle. On the second day there is another circle in addition to the earlier circle and so on. On the tenth day the tenth circle is clinched. Each circle stands for a Hindu deity. The first circle for example stands for Lord Ganesha. People in new robes are full of gaiety relishing ceremonial food such as pumpkin erissary, beet pachadi etc delighting in Onam songs, plays and dances. Onam folk songs are being sung through the generations. Many of them are sung in praise of Mahabali. This Onam folk song echoes in Dominic:

the golden rule of Maveli
. . . .
Equality prevailed in the society;
no lies, no crimes, no deceits;
and no cheat;
no poverty, no child death.
All were happy;

("Onam" 37-38)

Such songs are collectively called 'onapattu.' Onam dances include Kathakali, Kaikottikali, Thumbi thullal, Kummatti kali, Pulikali etc.

Spirited competitions, sports games and arts are familiar sights during Onam. Boat races, rowing in perfect rhythm singing boat songs are pageants of rare beauty in the world. Boat race or *vallam kal*i takes place among snake boats with more than 100 oarsmen in each boat rowing and singing at the same time. Nature also participates in the jubilee. Clear sky, bright sun, fragrance of flowers everywhere! Thus Dominic is adept in delineating Gods plenty in our enjoyment of the animal spirits and merrymaking loud with song and dance.

The festival is reminiscent of the golden age. Long time ago there was an Asura (demon) king named Mahabali. He founded a paradise upon earth. Everywhere there was abundance and abandon. No one was hungry, no one was poor. And love was universal. But Lord Vishnu the god of gods of Hindu pantheon outwitted the demon Mahavali and made him a prisoner. And the golden age went out of joints. Was it justified to imprison the great demon Mahabali who created heaven upon earth? Are gods just at all when the predicament of men is concerned?

Mahabali gets temporary release from his imprisonment to visit Kerala during Onam. Dominic says:

> Maveli visits on Onam;
> Fed up,
> he returns in tears.

("Onam" 38)

In short, below the surface of the great gaiety of Onam, there is the undercurrent of tears. Only three lines of the poem in a flash turn the merriment of Onam into a mournful song or a dirge. This is possible only when the pen is held by a master artist.

The wonderful festival Onam where joys and sorrows mingle takes place only in Kerala. Dominic says:

> My native State Kerala
> blessed with equable climate
> and alluring landscape
> crowned by the Sahyas
> she lies on the lap of Arabian Sea
> Multitudes of brooks and rivers
> flow through her veins
> Thousands of species of flora and fauna
> Six months long rainy season
> followed by summer bearable
> Autumn and winter fear to enter
> Tourists call it God's own country

("Multicultural Kerala" 161)

There have been regional novelists like Thomas Hardy of Wessex, Bibhuti Bhusan Bandyopadhyaya of Chhotonagpur, West Bengal. Dominic is a poet of a State. He is the poet of Kerala. He speaks of the multicultural Kerala. Approximately 54 percent of the people are Hindus, 26 percent of the people are Muslims and 18 percent of the people are Christians here. Thus it is a multi-religious society.

Chellamma Antharjanam, a seventy years old Hindu woman abandoned by her dear and near ones rushes to put her head on the railway track to make an end to her life. A young lady Resiya Beevi, mother of four kids and Muslim by religion rescues her and takes her to her house. She treats the old lady as her own mother. A Hindu woman, the old lady is a strict vegetarian. Resiya sees to that and bears all her expenses as long she lives. ("For the Glory of God" 108-109)

The Chattannoor Saint Mary's Church was getting ready for its annual festival. Christians, Hindus, Muslims--all were participants in the festival committee. Atul Krishnan, a Hindu boy lived opposite to the church. A motorbike accident killed him. The church cancelled the festival. The church cancelled booking of elephants and bands. This is the holy land of Kerala—Gods own land. ("An Ideal Festival" 213)

The Gods own Land is proud of great social workers, great leaders like E. K. Nayanar and she is very much proud of the child prodigy born to a trapeze tightrope performer.

> having no formal education
> surprised all as mental calculator
> from the tender age of three
> University scientists bowed their heads
> amazed at her skill at age of six
>
> ("A Tribute to Sakuntala Devi" 208)

It is Sakuntala Devi.

Gods own Land Kerala is blessed with untold wealth of flora and fauna. Jackfruits here serve as feast to birds and squirrels. The mango trees bear fruit for others. The coconut trees standing erect on lean tall foot are a marvel to all architects. But it is a pity that man is destroying Nature by raising dams and building airports. The poet sadly tells us:

> I can hear the scream of elephants, tigers,
> Boars, snakes and all wild animals
>
> ("I can Hear the Groan of Mother Earth" 229)

The forests of Kerala play hosts to Asian elephants, Bengal tigers, giant squirrels and variety of deer and leopards.

Wolfgang flew all the skies from Germany to Kerala at the sad silent call of plants and animals. And he has been long forty years in the dense forests of Kerala:

> Twenty species of snakes,
> fifteen types of amphibians,
> two twenty species of birds,
> sixty varieties of butterflies,
> two thousand kinds of plants,
>
> ("Wolfgang, the Messiah of Nature" 135)

To eye-witness the bounty of Nature in Kerala one had better visit Wagamon. One must reach there along steepish street running like anaconda. And at once loud cataracts, some like white paint and others like eternal curtains, eternal fallings will engross one's eyes and ears. Tall and thick pine trees support the firmament. Rolling green and pine leaves deck the ground with a carpet. The nights there are loud with cricket. ("Wagamon" 131)

If myths and legends have to be believed in, Kerala God's own land was once upon a time ruled by the great demon Mahabali. Abundance and abandon reigned in the country during the golden rule of Mahabali. But god Vishnu himself robbed the people of their happiness by deposing Mahabali. May be Vishnu felt that no *deus ex machina* should bring about peace and happiness among men who were once expelled from Eden by God the Father himself. People must rise up to heaven on their own through their karma.

But right now our angel poet a Mahabali visiting Kerala during Onam looking about with baleful eyes laments:

> Once God's own country with equable climate
> Rainy season for six months
> and mild summer for the rest of the year
> Blessed with brooks, rivers, lakes and greeneries
> Now people are crazy for pleasures and luxuries
> tumbled nature's balance and bounties
> resulting scanty rain and intolerable heat
> So where shall I free from this fretful land?
>
> ("Where shall I Flee from This Fretful Land" 210)

The poet Dominic is so much in love with his native land Kerala that he cannot migrate from here despite the fact that it is being turned into a wasteland. Dear Readers, Please allow us to extrapolate. Dominic as an Indo-English poet is widely known abroad. And maybe he got offers from abroad to serve there and stay there. But he will not leave his native State and country. Kerala is a State in the country of India. And Dominic's love for Mother India is the life blood that flows through the very veins of his poetical work. The very words mother, matha and ma are hallowed with Dominic. Because

> How shall I define mother's love?
> No lexicon term can convey it
> Inexpressible, indefinable, unfathomable
> immaculate, eternal and divine is maternal love!
>
> ("Maternal Attachment" 232-233)

On the Poet's Country, India

Dominic's ode to Mother India—"Victory to thee Mother India" (p. 92) opens with the paean:

> Victory to thee Mother India;
> for you did unite the races
> divided on religion,
> culture, language and colour.

The poem ends with:

> Tagore, Gandhi and Nehru
> were your great sons;
> no doubt, your womb
> will bear more great children,
> who will lift us from this trance
> and tether us back to the global home,
> and you will sleep on the lap
> fondled by your Mother World.

The poem is significant because it is aware of and proud of the heritage of the 19th century India.

> A hundred years back
> thy great son, Tagore
> sang in praise of you.
> Matha, you could rouse then
> the hearts of Punjab, Sind, Gujarat,
> Maratha, Dravida, Orissa and Bengal.

This poem not only echoes the national song but also speaks of the deep influence that Tagore cast upon Dominic. Tagore likened the Indian civilization with an ocean where the streams of different culture have mingled. Dominic is by the by a significant Tagore scholar. But Dominic is not a votary of raw nationalism. Our nationalism must pave the way to internationalism. Dominic dreams that our motherland should sleep on the lap fondled by mother World. Thus there is the vision of a World mother in whose lap all the nations of the world will gambol. A rare imagery of world mother where every culture, every religion, every language, every nation will find its home.

Chapter 2 - What Led the Poet to Write Poems?

So far we have discovered Dominic's mother, a glimpse of his childhood, his hometown, his native State, his country and his awareness as a member of the human race in the outline, from his poems. Of course we do not have his voter ID, Pan Card, Aadhaar Card etc. Hah Hah! But think of a poetical work without a poet. Impossible! Dominic is the speaker of the poems. He is the protagonist of the drama of his poetical works and they will gradually unfold the character called Dominic or the poet.

We must have a functional author of any verbal work. Otherwise we cannot make sense of it. When a cuckoo sings or a crow caws we do not focus on which crow caws or which cuckoo sings and we cannot make sense of it the way we make sense of human speech. But if we ever mistake a bird for a man crying, we at once respond to the same as we respond to the cry of a man. Think of Joseph Poorgrass in Thomas Hardy's *Far From the Madding Crowd* walking along a lonely path in the still of the night. He hears an owl crying—Whoo Whoo Whoo! He takes it for the voice of a man and, at once, he kneels down saying in all humility—"Joseph Poorgrass of Wetherbury, sir".

Hence, despite the fact that Roland Barthes has announced that there has been the death of the author, any book of poems must have an author. An author is one who has composed the poems. What are the poems? That which has been composed by the author. Thus true that the poems are there only for our eyes to read and ears to hear and our minds to judge. But unless they are felt to be written by a human speaker we would not decode them as we decode human language. So any speech whatever deemed to be human speech, poetry itself being a speech, has a speaker. And who is the speaker? He who has uttered the speech. And man being a metaphysical animal always seeks to know the speaker and his motive and intention lifting up the appearance of the poems or a pattern of words.

In fact, the poet is everywhere in the poem. Poetry is a thing seen through a personality—the poet. Hence in other words when we read the poetical works of X or Y or Dominic we read the world as seen through the eyes of Mr X or Mr Y or Mr Dominic. Poetry is the representation of the world in some way or other. We readers represent them in another way. When Barthes exclaimed that "the author is dead" what he meant thereby was that the reader is the final creator of the text. And of course a single text could multiply into as many texts as there are readers of the single text. Where is the text? It is not there in the printed matter. It is there in the mind of the reader. Plato posited that this world is a representation of the indeterminate reality. No representation can be accurate. Otherwise there cannot be any difference between the original and representation. If the original were alone and if there is an exact representation of the original there will be no aloneness of the original and the original will not be there. With Plato the reality as represented by the world is an illusion. The poets through the representation of the world take us farther away from the reality. Hence Plato banished the poets from his Republic. And no wonder that readers like the present one of Dominic would be summarily banished from his Republic as well.

Be that as it may, once we acknowledge the virtual existence of the author who is the protagonist in the drama of a poetical work and once we acknowledge the existence of a reader of a poetical work the reader is apt to ask: what led the author to compose poems?

What led Dominic to write poems? Unlike Sakuntala Devi, the "human computer" who started calculating at the age of three, Dominic did not forge verses in his infancy. His mother would be sometimes very angry with him. Once, when a child, Dominic fell from the swing and his mother chided him. ("Thodupuzha Municipal Park" 202) But Dominic the child did not have the occasion to implore his mother

> Mother mother pity take
> Never shall I verses make.

Dominic's first poem was composed when he was 48 years of age. Dominic himself dwells on how his first poem was written in his preface to his *Essential Readings* thus:

> One of my colleagues, Prof. George Joson, of the Department of Mathematics drowned in a river as he was driving back to his house at 11 pm on 14 May 2004. It was raining cats and dogs throughout the night, and the body was found out in the early morning frozen in the driver's seat of his car. . . . Joson was my intimate friend, living with his unemployed wife and three little daughters—resembling three angels—just two hundred metres away from my house. Thus my "bad heart"—heavy and brimming with grief, released the tension on paper after two days. (p. xvii)

The anecdote reminds us of Valmiki:

> A couple of Krauncha birds one day
> As they were busy in their love play
> The male one was hit by an arrow
> While the female cried out in sorrow
>
> This touched Valmiki's soft heart
> He cursed the hunter, in short

A future O hunter you'll never have
For killing a bird in the midst of love.
   (*Ramayana* by Rajaram Ramachandran, Bhaktivedanta Book Trust, 2007)

Valmiki cursed the hunter and cursed Death. Presently Valmiki exclaimed: What is it uttered by me! And the creator Brahma appeared before and told him that he had created *sloka* or poetry. With the craft of a poet he should delineate the life story of Rama.

On the 14th May 2004 Joson drowned. Next day, the day when Joson's body was buried, E. K. Nayanar, the Kerala Chief Minister who was very dear to Dominic died. And Dominic's first poem "In Memoriam George Joson" (p.1) was followed by "Long Live E. K. Nayanar." (p.3) These two poems won great acclaim from fellow teachers and goaded Dominic to write more and more. The fellow teachers were Brahma in this case. Brahma told Valmiki as to what to write about. And this role was played by a piece of paper in Dominic's situation:

> Hey poet, kindly heed to my plea
> before you thrust your pen
> into my bleeding heart
> Though I am a passive sheet of paper
> I have a soul as vibrant as yours
> Please don't vomit your trash
> through your volcanic missile
> The less you write the more we live
> the more our plant family lives
> Kindly write on the need of the day
> the necessity of conservation
> of plants and animals on earth
>
> ("On Conservation" 163)

Finally God Himself dictates him a poem: "Write My Son, Write" (pp. 74-87). It reminds one of Caedmon. Caedmon was an unlettered shepherd. Once God commanded him to sing in a dream. Waking up he sang. That was the true beginning of the Bible in Anglo Saxon language.

On the Elegies

As we have already observed, the death of a friend, George Joson, prompted Dominic's first poem, we had better read it with attention. The poem opens with the address to the dead soul:

> Why did you leave us so soon, dear Joson?
>
> ("In Memoriam George Joson" 1)

This is commonplace and human. Even though we do not die willingly, in most cases when someone dies we fancy that he has left us at his will. The dead body of Joson lies in front of the poet. But the poet employs *Arundhati-darsana-nyaya*

(Sanskrit term which stands for the process of moving from the known to the unknown), to infer a deeper truth from a visual imagery in the contingent:

> The most painful was the sight
> When your youngest kid,
> not knowing what has happened,
> kissed your face often
> and plucked flowers
> from your wreath;
> tossed them to her sisters weeping and screaming
>
> ("In Memoriam George Joson" 1)

The innocent child does not know what death is. But we the onlookers know what great loss and bereavement the little child faces without knowing. With the little child the father is not dead. He cannot die. The child tears the flowers from the wreath about his sleeping father's body and flings them at the weeping sisters. There could be no more pathetic a sight. The poet ironically posits that just as a child plays with the wreaths about a dead body so does God play with human life.

> As flies to wanton children we are to th' gods,
> They kill us for their sport.
>
> (*King Lear* Act 4, scene 1, 32–37)

And there is no escape from it. "When He comes with His chariot, / none can say—"wait"." ("In Memoriam George Joson" 1) Who else is God but Death? Mark you, Death does not come in his chariot. Death comes with his chariot. Chariot is a kind of fast moving carriage. Think of Elijah in Old Testament. A chariot of fire drawn by the horses of fire carried Elijah to heaven. And surely the chariot has come to Joson and death has no sting. But we are mortals living in the contingent governed by our habits and limited knowledge. We weep even when one leaves us for a journey to heaven. Our attachment is perhaps to blame for this. It blinds us.

The four lines from the 17th fytte to the 21st fytte shift the focus.

> Now we understand the mystery of your ever being fast--
> fast in your words;
> fast in your walk;
>
> ("In Memoriam George Joson" 1)

This clearly brings home the personality of Joson to the readers. Joson speaks fast. So unless you are all ears to him you cannot follow him. He walks fast. So unless you walk fast you cannot walk with him. These are his humour. These could be praises of Joson. But his qualities could be at the same time his nemesis. He has been "FAST UNTO DEATH." ("In Memoriam George Joson" 1) Must be he drove very fast during the fateful night on the 14th of May.

Thus there is a narrative. There was a learned professor whose name was Joson. He was fast in everything, fast in speech, fast in action. One night he was a little late. He drove fast homeward. Flood water drowned the road. Joson could have been a little cautious and slow. May be the car skidded and he drowned. The poet went to pay last respects to his dead friend Joson and saw how helpless was the unemployed Joson's wife with her three children. It is ironical that Joson drove fast only to meet them and Joson thereby drifted far away from them. The narration however sets the time sequence in a different manner. At the outset we find Joson dead. The poet asks: "Why did you leave us so soon, dear Joson?" ("In Memoriam George Joson" 1) Any death makes the thoughtful contemplate on the import of life. At the outset the poet asked: Why did you leave us so soon, dear Joson? As if man is responsible for his death. Is he? After a moment's reflection the poet murmured to himself that "We are all puppets in His hands, / dancing to His various tunes." ("In Memoriam George Joson" 2) But finally the poet resigns himself to the will of God:

> We are all
> bound by His will
> to be here
> to be away.
>
> ("In Memoriam George Joson" 1-2)

Men must endure their going, hence even as their coming hither. "Ripeness is all."--That is Shakespeare's. With Dominic "We are all puppets in His hands." The reader asks—Is it?

Thus the first poem in Dominic's poetic career flings before us an overwhelming question. Dominic lifts and drops an overwhelming question in our plate. The poet is one who serves foods for thought to the readers.

On the 14th May Joson passed away. Joson was the personal friend of Dominic. It was a personal loss of Dominic. Before the loss of Joson and the grief thereof could be met foursquare, the people of Kerala were plunged into mourning at the death of E. K. Nayanar, a leader of the masses. A vast surging sea of humanity followed wailing and weeping on Nayanar's last journey. No rain could stop them; no sleep could retreat them. Nature herself seemed to participate in the mourning. Dominic also became the part of mourning. Thus mourning for personal loss mingled with the mourning of the masses for a general loss became sublimated. And when the poet exclaims in his address to Nayanar,

> Your absence from amidst us
> shows your presence among the stars.
> You are our polestar
> who saves us from the Darkness.
>
> ("Long Live E. K. Nayanar" 4)

does not the reader find Joson too effulgent in the skies? Thus the poem on the death of E. K. Nayanar is a sequel to the poem on the death of Joson. Both are elegies. Both are songs of bereavement and could be sung with a flute. True to literary type they raise questions about destiny, justice and fate. They are Christian elegies and proceed from sorrow and misery to hope and happiness. Because with Christianity through death one passes from life to eternity.

There is a third elegy in "Ammini's Lament" (p. 46). Ammini is a baby name among Keralites. It is a cat. It has three children--kittens. Two of them are missing. Absence and death are metaphorically synonymous. When the child is absent for long don't we think that he or she must have been killed? If someone is dead is s/he not absent and will s/he not remain absent for all time to come? And think of Ammini's anguish when she finds two of her kitten missing.

> Ammini can't forget
> even after ten days
> the loss of her darlings.
> Day in and day out
> she wanders on all sides
> seeking the twins of her triplet.
> . . . .
> Ammini's changed a lot;
> no greed for food;
> no frolic with her son.
> How long will she go on wailing?

("Ammini's Lament" 46)

Ammini's incessant cries echo in the premises. Her wails remind the poet of the laments of Gandhari at the sight of the hecatomb of Kurukshetra. Gandhari had lost hundred sons in the battles of Kurukshetra. When we find our dear ones dead, we miss them. What is death but our dear ones missing? The simile that compares Ammini's sorrows with those of Gandhari also throws a flood light on the epic Mahabharata. If we agree that God himself contrived the great war of Kurukshetra, what benefit was derived from the same? On the contrary, the wails of Gandhari and other mothers echoed at the hecatomb called Kurukshetra. The wails were as heart rending as the laments of a cat mother echoing in the household of the poet in quest of her missing children. And think of the cat mother refusing food after it lost her two children. Does it not describe the mental predicament of the mothers who lost their children in Kurukshetra and who lose their children in battlefields?

Earlier men had direct communication with animal world and plant world. In Shakespeare's Macbeth, the weird sisters or the Wyrd sisters who can see into the future are directly in touch with Graymalkin and Paddock. The Wyrd sisters are wiser than us and Dominic is a poet with their esoteric wisdom. The poet reminds us of the fact that animals are as affectionate as humans. Neither wealth nor learning nor power but love and affection make a man noble. The same nobility is found among animals.

Ammini's lament has been put in a frame. Her kittens have not been dead. They were sold away. This is child trafficking. In fact Ammini's lament is more a lament than an elegy. Lament is a genre in its own right that gives a passionate tongue to acute grief. And the lament in this poem is on two levels. It was the poet himself who had sold the kitten of Ammini. He puts himself in the dock in front of the bench of his own conscience. The poem is a monologue. It opens with the poet lamenting:

> How to expiate
> the merciless sin
> committed to my cat?
>
> ("Ammini's Lament" 46)

Shakespeare's dramas such as *Macbeth* portray such so called villains who are capable of great passions and griefs. Dominic here reminds one of Macbeth who realized that the thane of Cawdor had killed sleep and Macbeth would sleep no more. But it is a pity when we compare ourselves with Macbeths or the poet we feel that we are postcards. We are not capable of great passions and laments. We have no conscience as it were. The poem "Ammini's Lament" depicts the poet as human in his sorrow mickle. The poet as we have already observed compares the grief of Ammini with that of Gandhari. Gandhari curses Krisna. And does not the cat curse the poet? This puts forward a philosophical question. The insects cannot recognize the multi-cellular ones or animals. But an animal can recognize the insects. Similarly an animal cannot recognize man the so called rational animal though man can recognize an animal. A dog cannot recognize man as man. But a man can recognize a dog. Just as we do harms to animals and the animals might curse us, so we do curse the gods. And are the gods who bring misfortunes upon us some supermen whom we do not recognize although who know us?

The poems also raise questions as to jurisprudence. Is not killing an animal or stealing a child animal from its mother as serious a crime as the offence of killing a man or trafficking in children?

"An Elegy on My Ma" (p. 89) stands out among the poems composed by Dominic. Dominic's mother is dead. But her face is ever fresh in the mind of the poet. Dominic gazes at her face inwardly. She is smiling. Ripples from the smile of the face stream down to raise a tsunami in the mind of the poet. The poet's bereaved heart burns. The glow in the eyes of the mother darts like a lightening to the poet's burning heart. Although the poet does not undertake to describe how his mother looked like, the glow of her darting eyes and her smile makes her alive before our mind's eyes. Does it not suggest that wherever she went she illuminated and that she braved all the odds of life with a smile?

Time is the best healer. With the passage of time whatever terrible a grief might be, fades. The pangs of loss become blunted. But ironically enough the poet's sorrow increases day after day since the day she went into the earth. Even many years after the mother's demise, the poet is not reconciled with the death of the mother. It seems to the poet as if she died presently.

The poet recollects how hard she worked even before her marriage. She worked in the farm and she never let her six children feel the chill of penury. But could her children serve her in the selfsame way? The poet asks:

> How can your cent percent
> match with our ten percent?
>
> ("An Elegy on My Ma" 90)

None can reciprocate for what s/he receives from his or her mother. The poet exclaims:

> Truly mother's love
> is the purest love
> and divine love.
>
> ("An Elegy on My Ma" 90)

We have seen how Ammini, a cat wept for her two missing children and gave up food and drink. The poet also has the heart of a mother. Just as a mother looks upon her baby as the gift of God, so does Dominic look upon a kitten received from his friend as God's gift. We can imagine with what happiness he received the gift of a kitten from his friend. It was a gift of God through his friend. No other poet, to the best of the knowledge of the present reader, has looked upon a subhuman species with so much love and affection. Although a cat is a cat, it is as dear to Dominic as a human child. He sees the manifestation of God in her face. He hears the voice of God in the mews of the cat. And when the mews of the cat echoes in his house he hears God in that. And an untold bliss fills his heart.

The mother of a poet, Dominic loves all children, be they human or animal. And Dominic leaves the kitten in the car of one of his friends by mistake. And the kitten flees through the window of the car. And Dominic misses the kitten and wails as piteously as the cat mother Ammini lamented who had lost her two kittens. Dominic muses: Is she living or dead? / Is she seeking still her mother ("Attachment" 100).

We cannot but recite the hymn to maternal love in the poem "Mother's Love":

> Maternal love, love sublime
> Inexplicable, unfathomable
> Noblest of all emotions
> Visible both on human beings
> and other beings
> Both on domestic animals
> and wild animals
> Mother feeding babies
> seeking food for them
> with much labour
> She eats only after

> they are fed or
> leaving portions for them

The Durgasaptasati of the Markandeya purana however observes in this context that men bring up children with the hope that the children will look after them in their old age. But look at the birds. They fly about thousand times a day and carry grains in their beaks to feed their little ones despite the fact that they are hungry. But once the little ones are capable of flying they fly away without taking notice of their parents. The parents also do not lament for the children who fly away. But even when we try to do our duties to our parents while they give us cent percent we can give them ten percent. Dominic in his elegy on his mother addresses her departed mother:

> Ma, I couldn't be
> at your bedside
> when you murmured
> throughout night
> "Call my children;
> ask them sing."
>
> ("An Elegy on My Ma" 90)

"Whatsoever a man soweth, that shall he also reap" (Galatians VI, *King James Version*). That is the Bible, the highest voice under the scene. We who could not perform our duties to our mothers must address our dead mothers and cry:

> What would be our fate, Ma,
> when we become old as you?
>
> ("An Elegy on My Ma" 91)

When we were children we used to hear our parents saying that they obeyed their parents and performed their duties to their parents. But they were afraid that we would not do our duties in the self same way. True. Now we also tell the same to our children who have grown up. Dominic also addresses his dead mother and says:

> Ma, you were never
> deserted by your children.
> What would be our fate, Ma,
> when we become old as you?
>
> ("An Elegy on My Ma" 91)

These lines are very eloquent. We have caught Dominic off his guard. Firstly it is here that Dominic gives vent to real anxieties. He is afraid whether our children will look after us when we grow very old. This is a feeling rather strange in the realm of poetry. The poet may give a tongue to our anxieties with the shape of things to come in the economic realm or political realm and so on. Poets might condemn the moral standard of the youth. But where is the poet who fears that he would not be looked after by his children when he grows old? This shows that Dominic is different. Secondly Dominic is as old as the present reader and gives a tongue to the anxieties of the present reader. We pray that other readers should be free from such anxieties. Besides, Dominic writes his poem exactly as he talks to his dear and near ones. Thirdly, it follows that Dominic does not have any choice for themes in poetry. Anything could be the theme of poetry ranging from the stars in the firmament to a bathroom. That is an aesthetics. Finally we must agree that whether we like it not, his poems are stamped with his real feelings and emotions.

"An Elegy on My Ma" gives a lengthy description of the sufferings of the mother presently before death. The lassix tablets are still on the table. They remind the poet of the untold suffering of the mother. When she laboured for breath, she cried for these tablets. Dominic remembers:

> Your sleepless nights,
> sitting and wheezing,
> when we were fast asleep,
> . . . .
> long six years,
> bewailing often
> "Why doesn't God
> call me back?"
> and finally bed-ridden
> for a long week
> with no food
> but a little water—
>
> ("An Elegy on My Ma" 90)

Does it not remind us of the cat mother who gave up food and water? It is said the mother murmured throughout the night—"call my children and ask them sing." Did she have a premonition of death? Or did she see death visiting her with a coffin. Because she was heard to whisper "Remove the box." This is how indeed we speculate when we muse over the last thoughts of our dying mother or the dear ones. When she suffered from breathing problem she whispered "God take me back." When death visited her with a coffin, she whispered "Remove the box." Dominic wonders whether she was reluctant to leave her children and the world. And finally she asked her children to sing a requiem. This wavering of thoughts of the dying mother makes her character human and lively before us. We wonder whether death has its strings. Did not death rescue the mother from her sufferings that continued for long six years? And again perhaps one feels reluctant to leave the much loved worldly life of ours where three parts are pain.

True that only these four or five elegiac poems touch upon the battle for life in the face of death but the major corpus of Dominic's poems are directly or indirectly associated with life in death or death in life. And most of his poems are heavily weighed with the cargo of laments. Elegy is their leitmotif. But we will have a glimpse of them later in a different context.

The elegy on his mother is a robust portrayal of a woman fighting hard for survival throughout her life. Early in her life she lost her parents. Even before marriage she worked hard to bring up her brothers. Marriage did not give her any relief on the physical and economic plane. She bore six children and worked in the farms. She lived two hundred percent–hundred percent in the kitchen and the household and hundred percent working hard outdoor, walking across the brambles.

> Dawn to dusk
> worked on the farm;
> Made the field fertile
> with gallons of sweat.

("An Elegy on My Ma" 89)

Dominic said that although they were six, no one starved, no one felt the pangs of poverty. And as we already know, the son of a farmer, Dominic has climbed up to the higher echelon of the society. He got the highest possible education available in India and he retired as a professor. Dominic seems to be very proud of his farmer mother. She has been heroic in her battle for life. And hers is an instance of life in death. She asked to sing beside her deathbed at the moment of her bidding adieu to the world and us. She reminds us of the useful toil and the short simple annals of the poor. She reminds us of some mute inglorious Milton, some Cromwell guiltless of the country's crime.

Elegy as a genre commonly laments the death of a person. Consequently it could dwell on the last battle of life against the impending death. Dominic excels in vividly describing the situation.

A sheep addresses man and tells him:

> I have seen with my eyes
> and heard with my ears
> the last cries of my parents.
>
> When they became old
> you cut their heads
> and ate their flesh.

("A Sheep's Wail" 8)

Indeed a child fleeing from modern-day Syria might address the murderer of its parents in the selfsame parole. Is there any big difference between a sheep and the child of a man? Before we approach the delineation of man's struggle for breath in the face of death we had better look at the live picture of a few animals dying. Dominic is fond of cats. And he used to have pet cats. Ammini is a baby-name in Malayalam. And Dominic has a cat christened Ammini. There are two poems one after another on Ammini's laments and Ammini's demise. They are companion poems. Read together, they could be a narrative where Ammini is the central character. In Ammini's lament, Ammini misses two of its kittens. Absence of dear and near ones could be as much loss as one's loss of one's kin into the jaws of death. Indeed the death of a dear and near one implies his absence for all time to come. And just as we men cannot bear such absence of our dear and near ones so do cats. The kittens are missing for long ten days.

> Ammini can't forget
> even after ten days
> the loss of her darlings.
> Day in and day out
> she wanders on all sides
> seeking the twins of her triplet. ("Ammini's Lament" 46)

Presently Ammini changes a lot.

> no greed for food;
> no frolic with her son. ("Ammini's Lament" 46)

The poet asks:

> How long will she go on wailing? ("Ammini's Lament" 46)

If we did not know that Ammini is a cat, the description could be deemed as that of a bereaved mother of a human child. Thus Ammini, the cat is no different from any Ammini, the human mother of a human child. So that is the indicator of Ammini the cat. If Ammini's demise is deemed to be the continuation of Ammini's story, then it narrates how misfortunes in her life come in a train. She is poisoned to death. The poet notes:

> Poisoned to death
> Ammini's struggle
> for breath and water;
> our effort in vain
> to keep her alive;
> and her final adieu
> without even a sound; ("Ammini's Demise" 47)

Poetry often functions to revive the memory of the readers' past experience. The law of association reminds the present reader of the silent groans of a child who softly told his mother---Ma I will not live any longer! Ammini dies without a sound.

A neighbour of Dominic poisons four cats at a time. A massacre of cats! All the four die.

> One after other,
> all the four died,
> struggling hysterically

> for water and breath,
> soft velvety fur
> drenched in saliva
> and excrement.
>
> ("Massacre of Cats" 94)

We can see, as it were, the cats struggling hysterically for water and breath live. This tremor of life has been juxtaposed with the lifeless saliva and excrement. Saliva and excrement could repel the readers. But when our dear ones die amidst saliva and excretion our tears well forth. What is ugly turns into something very lovable at the magic touch of Dominic's Muse. This lovely heart rending scene is charged with the aesthetics of cruelty that dazes our conscious mind and appeals to our subconscious mind to cleanse the same.

"To My Deceased Cats" opens with:

> "Lo, our Rocky is struggling;
> God, is he departing us?"
> Pussy cat cried to his friends.
> "Has cruel man poisoned him?" ("To My Deceased Cats" 136)

Yes cruel man poisoned him. Rocky groans and gasps. But he has no complaint against the man who poisoned him.

> Rocky ended with a loud wail;
> his body shuddered and died. ("To My Deceased Cats" 137)

A pathetic sight indeed! The struggle for life against approaching death, always a kinaesthetic imagery etched by Dominic shocks our bodies and minds violently.

Not only cats are poisoned to death by man, man equally dismembers the limbs of Nature:

> Siachen glacier feeding several rivers
> irrationally axed and dug ("Siachen Tragedy" 156)

Here Siachen glacier feeding several rivers is human as it were and it is irrationally axed and dug.

The celestial fire that burnt in the heroic mother of Dominic exerted enormous influence on the poet Dominic. And they give us the clue to his boundless love, sympathy, reverence for motherhood, wives, daughters and sisters; in short for womanhood, which is littered all over the works of Dominic.

While a lavish wedding feast in full swing, Dominic could see:

> . . . two ragged girls outside
> struggling with the dogs in the garbage bin. ("A Nightmare" 6)

The sad melody and accents of Iambic as we found in Gray recur here. It is a pity that in the society of ours we men treated our fellowmen often as street dogs and cats. Think of Browning's Duke in the poem "My Last Duchess." He killed his wife just as one would kill a wild horse. Her only offence was to smile at the sunrise and to smile at sunset, to smile at any person with whom she crossed roads. The Duke commanded her to smile only at him.

On the Issues of Women, Parents and Old Age

When we talk of poets of our time we must say Dominic is a rare type of a poet. He is truthful and honest. He does not present his poems in borrowed robes at a meet where poetry is feasted upon. In a nightmare Dominic sees:

> See, what a mansion that double storied edifice!
> Luxury rooms, lawn and swimming pool;
> An old man and his wife resided there;
> sitting at the phone with sighs and moans,
> longed for the calls of the sons abroad.

("A Nightmare" 6)

The same imagery has been elaborated in the poem "Gayatri's Solitude" (15). Gayatri is now eighty two years old. She was widowed at thirty five; mother of five children--three sons and two daughters all in the States. The pointedness and details of description as in "widowed at thirty five, mother of five children, three sons and two daughters," remind one of Keats and Yeats. Keats shut the La belle dame sans merci with kisses four. But he failed to blind the reality of the day to day world—the beautiful woman without mercy. The same pointedness of description and sometimes statistics has been handled by Dominic to convince us of the ugly face of reality where the pale princes and pale warriors, a mother at the age of eighty-two who was widowed in her thirties and who brought up five children against all odds heroically is now in thrall--an old age home. The nine and fifty swans at Coole in Yeats seek to prove that hearts do not grow old. And Dominic observes:

> An old lily flower
> pale and faded.
> Dawn to dusk,
> sitting in an armchair,
> looking at the far West,
> longing for her childrens' calls,
> she remains in solitude

("Gayatri's Solitude" 15)

An imagery of loneliness and alienation, which is time and again one wonders whether our parents and our near and dear ones will wait for phone calls leaning on the gold bar of heaven in the self same way.

The eighty two years old lady recalls:

> How lucky were her parents!
> Lived happy, died happy;

> always with their children;
> sons, daughters,
> daughters-in-law,
> sons-in-law,
> a dozen grand children,
> a house full of mirth.
>
> ("Gayatri's Solitude" 15)

Whither is fled that visionary gleam, the glory and the dream? Dear Poet, this disappearance of the glory and the dream is not always because of the self-centredness of the children nowadays. You yourself could not turn up at the bedside of your dying mother. Capitalism and globalization are to be blamed. The young do not get employment opportunities in their native place or in the native State or in the native country.

The more I read Dominic I am carried away more by his courage to speak. I am seventy. I have two children. Dominic speaks on behalf of countless parents like us. It is we the parents who have given birth to our children and it is we who looked after them when they were helpless babies and it is we who sought hard for their employment. But it is a pity that:

> Parents in eighties and nineties
> needing bed rest and medication
> admitted in hospitals by children
> When asked to pay the medicine bills
> desert them and disappear for ever
> Some are dropped on roadside
> Some even in thick forests
>
> ("Parents Deserted" 240)

Dear young readers, Will you blame us for begetting children? Damn your Malthus!

> Proton, electron; positive, negative;
> Male, female; made for each other.
> Pains and pleasures: God's own gifts.
> . . . .
> Instincts divine, divine pleasures;
> who can abstain them?
> . . . .
> Connubial bliss,
> heavenly happiness;
> merging of two souls;
> fulfilment of His plans. (
>
> "Connubial Bliss" 13)

God's plan is to herald Life's march in the existence. Of course, the parents must not look upon their children as their property. The parents are mere agents in giving fillip to the flow of life in its march as willed by God. If they look upon the children as their property they are fools. Because we men could not have offspring of our own. We are not the cause of the existence. And we cannot rein the flow of the system at our will. This is perhaps an indirect comment on the present rage on population control. Since man has not initiated procreation and since he cannot stop the process of procreation he cannot have right on children. In fact man has no right over anything in the universe. He is a product of a system and he had better flow with the system without any ego unless it is the ego to serve the system and serve God's will. Dominic reminds us that during old age:

> The monarch of yesterday,
> feels humbled today.
> . . . .
> Today's torturer
> tomorrow's victim;
> we live with ironies. ("Old Age" 35)

Dominic warns us however that despite the fact that we do not own our children, in the sense that one owns a movable property in the conventional sense, we must not let our children be reckless:

> Never dig your graves as Dhritarastra did ("Parental Duty" 239)

Dominic observes that it is the duty of the parents to become role models of their children. That is flowing like autumns leaf:

> Best is to be models to your children
> Leading lives of dharma and karma ("Parental Duty" 239)

Does Dominic thereby remind us:

> Today's torturer
> Tomorrow's victim; (?) ("Old Age" 35)

At the same time one asks what it is like to perform dharma and karma in old age. Well, dear readers, between you and me and off the record, Dominic is now a retired man. His children are well established. Now he devotes himself to spread the commonsense philosophy and the voice of God as heard by himself to make the much loved world of ours lovelier.

When men stand in long queue before the wine shop like ants in a line before their hole:

> A similar queue is found on the other side,
> where poor women wait for their rations. ("A Nightmare" 6)

A little girl complains:

> Ma, why didn't God create me a little more beautiful? ("Beauty" 12)

With the heart of a mother, Dominic tells us:

> Only spiritual beauty gives eternal joy.
> My dear lass, be like the sun,
> brightening this dark world with your inner beauty. ("Beauty" 12)

Many of the poems of Dominic are dramatic lyrics reminiscent of Browning.

Helen is a student who takes down notes in her class faster than a typewriter. Although she is blind she is the light of the class. Indeed light illuminates everything. But does the light see itself?

> She is the light of the class,
> light of the family,
> light of the village,
> . . . .
> Light fighting against darkness,
> Eternally! Hopefully! Surely!
>
> ("Helen and her World" 22-23)

This is an instance of death in life. An instance of oxymoron--a girl blind though is the light of the village. The repetition of the word light here is time and again. We remember "Pale warriors, death-pale were they all" in Keats. "La Belle Dame Sans Merci" has them in the thrall of darkness. Helen is the antagonist who brings light to them. In fact any speech, be it a poem or a story or an essay is a discourse. It begins only after another speech id clinched up. And we are sure Dominic's poems will have verbal responses from myriad ends. And this discourse, by me Mukhopadhyaya, has begun where Dominic ended his speech. Mark you, how the repetition of light here in Dominic does away with the gloom in the repetition of the word pale in Keats. And invest the poem with Dantesque imagination.

Language as such exerts power over the listeners and the readers. Aristotle speaks of three ways of persuasion in ethos, pathos and logos. So far we came by pathos in Dominic's poems. But his "International Women's Day" is an instance of logos loaded with reason and data.

> International Women's day;
> celebrations all over the world;
> meetings held;
> programmes chalked out;
> promises showered;
> fund allotted;
> celebrities honoured;
> her praises sung hoarse
> coarse in her life's course
> mockery's rhetoric in these celebrations!
>
> ("International Women's Day" 26)

The International Women's Day is celebrated in all its grandeur. But the apparent glitter and the grandeur of the celebration are at bottom hollow sham.

The poem begins at a climax. And then the anticlimax sets in. The celebration is a game for the elite in the society. The lot of women hasn't changed a micron from what it was earlier.

> Women is the game!
> Birth to death,
> an instrument of lust   ("International Women's Day" 26)

Her birth is an ill omen. And the society sees no guilt in foeticide. If mothers are thus humiliated, there is no life. If we do not let mothers to be born we will checkmate the flow of life. Gender discrimination in childhood is found everywhere. Priority is given to the brother. His left over is the grub of the sister. She has no toys to play. She always envies her brother. When mom and her dad love him she gets only reproaches. She is seldom educated and always dependent:

> slave to her husband,
> servant to her in-laws.
> Bears the burden of her birth;
> lives for her children
> . . . .
> Has no place in politics:
> councils, assemblies, parliaments,
> . . . .
> she has no right
> to enter her father's abode;
> no place in clergy.
> She is always the Other.   ("International Women's Day" 27)

There is no better poem on the state of women today in the world. But we must humbly seek to point out that earlier the women were not so unfortunate. Dominic's mother herself worked both indoor and outdoor and sustained her family, because in the works afield, there was not that wide gender difference. When technology and modern offices showed up, when capitalism had on its full sway over the society the women were sent to the kitchen. Because the common run of men cannot give equal education to men and women. The West is at heart patriarchal. Milton himself observes that while God the Father is a God of Adam, Adam is a God of Eve. And the life of Milton as delineated by Dr. Johnson tells us how Milton's wife had to be on her knees before Milton and his friends at her father's house. Thereafter only she could return to Milton. No wonder when the Anglo Saxons, the race of Milton, came to India to rule, they would give employment only to male. Be that as it may, the poem "International Women's Day" ends in a hymn to motherhood.

> Venerable is women,
> for she is your mother;
> she is your sister;

> she is your wife;
> she is your guide;
> she is your teacher;
> she is your nurse;
> and above all,
> she is your angel.
>
> ("International Women's Day" 27)

You will not find any other poet in Indian English literature who is as respectful to women and motherhood.

"Laxmi's Plea" is another dramatic lyric of great power and force. The poem opens with a wedding occasion amidst jocundity in a jolly hall. Rekha's wedding today. Rekha is a colleague of Laxmi, junior by ten years. Laxmi is in two minds--to be or not to be in the wedding hall. Why is Laxmi so shaky to join a wedding ceremony? At the wedding hall Laxmi meets her colleagues. Laxmi is single at thirty three. Why is she not married yet? Is she very ugly to look at? No. She looks very handsome. She is a lamp to any house. Of course plenty of proposals appeared with tea before many young men. Laxmi tells the poet

> None complained my looks.
> "What's the dowry?" ("Laxmi's Plea" 30)

And there ends all her hopes. Let us hear from Laxmi herself:

> Father died when I was ten;
> mother bed-ridden with cancer;
> a thatched house in five cents,
> an elder sister married off.
> My meagre salary two thousand
> hardly meets our food and medicine.
> . . . .
> Leave me alone;
> leave me single. ("Laxmi's Plea" 30)

Aside the poet murmurs:

> A lamp destined to burn out ("Laxmi's Plea" 30)

Look at the woman in the slum. Mother is bed ridden. Drunken husband will come at night to resume beats and kicks. ("What a Birth" 42) Dominic excels in dramatic lyrics. Earlier men and women worked together in the field. Capitalism drove the women to the kitchen from outdoor. Men rule in the world outdoor. Now women are also trying to have a space outdoor. Better late than never. And there is a woman who is sitting for an examination to wrest a place outdoor for survival. She is a married woman. She has a child. Sitting in the examination hall she can hear the cry of her child for the breast milk. What shall the woman do? What shall the mother do? Will she leave the examination hall to breastfeed the child or will she continue in the examination hall for two more hours? ("Cry of my

Child" 55) Hamlet is the prince of Denmark. His father is dead mysteriously. Whether he should probe into the death of his father is rather a question pertaining to the intellect and his princely status and so on. But think of a mother sitting in an examination hall hearing the call of her starved babe. True that she does not become the heroine of a noble tragedy. But the to be or not to be of the mother is far more engrossing than the to be or not to be of Hamlet. It involves not only the questions of economic security, it involves two throbbing bodies--one of the young mother, another of the little baby and they throw up life and death questions more immediate than those of Hamlet and more real than those of Hamlet to us the ordinary men. Dominic seems to have opened fresh pastures of poetry never attempted before in prose or rhyme.

And think of the girl child that is pining for her mother's breast. The poet smiles at the infant on her mother's shoulder. But the baby does not smile back. Her mother's appearance foretells the infant's lot.

> Born to poor parents,
> how thorny would be
> the path of her life!
> She is yet to toddle;
> But I (the poet) could vision
> the blood oozing from
> her soft feet.   ("Musings from an Infant's Face" 115)

With the poet the gory future of the infant is in the present.

> Being a female,
> . . . .
> abuses and tortures,
> will come in battalions
> . . . .
> Lame and tottering
> she will struggle along
> till she reaches
> her terminus, death.   ("Musings from an Infant's Face" 115-116)

It is not the fatal flaw nor the Nemesis that is responsible for the doom of these human children. Thanks to the inequality in the society, poverty makes Everywoman heroic!

Thanks to the food technology, artificial food:

> Parents are very sad,
> for little daughter has period:
> hormonic chicken daily food.   ("Nature Weeps" 119)

And there is another pen-picture of a woman's heroic struggle for survival:

> All eyes were fixed on the sky.
> A woman on a tall thorny tree;

> sharp spines covering
> trunk, branches and twigs.
> Standing on a bamboo ladder,
> a score feet high,
> shaming men she's
> felling thorny branches;
> support trees for pepper cuttings.
> When few men risk
> such hazardous labour,
> necessity goaded her
> to fight against fate.   ("Resolution" 120)

The reader wonders who is responsible for the fate of the like of her. In heroic poetry and romances and tragedies we have seen people going off to death in an attitude; beautiful ladies and fat bellied beaus looking upon them from the veranda. Life is really thrilling for those who act its glory and for those who see its romance. But they pale beside the real battles of life as waged by the lady climbing the thorny tree. Is there anyone among us the readers who cries "To arms, to arms, to war against a sea of troubles?" Dominic is one of those few poets who transports the readers to the melting mood.

Aeschylus wrote seventy to ninety tragedies. Seven tragedies of Sophocles survive out of 100 plays. Some 19 plays of Euripides survive. The tragedies written by Corneille or by Racine or by Shakespeare do pale before the tragedies composed by the capitalist system and the real life. Dominic's poetry drives us out from the cinema hall to witness what life is like. The mirror cracks from side to side. The glass house is shattered with thundering bang. Is there any Red Cross knight Sir Lancelot to take up our cause?

The part three of the poem "Multicultural Harmony" sums up the predicament of women in India:

> Her birth is an ill omen
> Millions are butchered
> before they are born
> Parents receive her
> as burden to family   ("Multicultural Harmony" 151)

Her brother is sent for school. But she must spend her life in the kitchen. She must live on the left over of her brother after her brother eats. She cannot choose her spouse. Often she is raped by her husband.

> Feeding of children
> falls on her shoulders
> Sacrifices her health
> for entire family
> Her struggle starts
> from early morning

> fights with utensils
> in the kitchen
> . . . .
> She is born with a cry
> goes on crying and crying
> till she reaches
> her destination death. ("Multicultural Harmony" 152)

Dominic finds women exploited everywhere--in families, institutions, societies, nations, politics and religion. Dominic asks:

> Why can't women be priests
> in churches, mosques and temples? ("Multicultural Harmony" 152)

Dominic observes that such discrimination between male and female does not exist among the animals. If equality were the criterion of civilization, are not animals more civilized than men? We men look upon women as commodity. We look at them with lascivious eyes as if we go about window shopping.

The Economics of the Poet

My learned fellow readers, some of them, may have been bored with my exegesis of Dominic's poetry as it is the exegesis of statement poetry. Statement poetry always tries to say something beyond a poetic theme or motif. In other words my learned fellow readers who have worked hard in the laboratory of literature and literary criticism may be apparently disappointed with Dominic because there is neither symbolism nor surrealism nor other tropes of poetic art. But one wonders whether there could be language at all without symbols and symbolism. Symbol according to Peirce is a sign where the sign relates to its object alone by means of convention. Well the married Bengalee women put on vermilion on the parting of hair. Vermilion on the parting of the hair is a symbol. Let us recall "Resolution"

> All eyes were fixed on the sky,
> A woman on a tall thorny tree;
> sharp spines covering
> trunk, branches, twigs
> Standing on a bamboo ladder,
> a score feet high,
> shaming men she's
> felling thorny branches; ("Resolution" 120)

This is clear representation of a woman climbing a tree for earning bread. But is not the tree, the tree of life and hence thorny? Thus the thorny tree is a symbol. And of course the poem could be read as a symbolist one that evokes horror in our minds.

An Elegy on My Ma gives us a vivid pen-picture of a mother working in the farm making the field fertile with gallons of sweat. The mother is the mother of civilization who laboured hard and taught men to cultivate. She is the symbol of the right economic activity—cultivation being the only economic activity.

In every production of new wealth some amount of wealth is destroyed out of necessity. The wealth destroyed must be subtracted from the wealth produced. The difference is net wealth produced. If the new wealth is in excess of the destroyed wealth, the excess should be deemed as net increase in wealth or net product. The physiocrats rightly observed that net product was confined to one class of production namely agriculture. Do away with the pollution the agriculturist produces more than what he or she produces. What other class of producers do is to transfer or to replace the product of agriculture. Neither the manufacturer produces anything of worth. What he does is to combine or modify the raw material. Industry is sterile. It does not produce any extra wealth.

True that industry and commerce might bring more gains than the production of food grains. But gains are gained and not produced. Two horses and two asses are not four but two horses and two asses. GDP earned from agriculture and GDP earned from entertainment industry should not be classed together to compute the GDP. Think of the world without food. Can the entertainment industry continue even for a day? Can Lata Mangeshkar sing anymore? Agriculture does possess the power of sustaining and creating forces of life, whether vegetable or animal. The fruits of the earth are given by God while the products of arts are wrought by man who is powerless to create (*A History of Economic Doctrines* by Charles Gide and others translated by R Richards George G Harrap, London, 1949, page 34) The agriculturists need house to live in, clothes to wear, and implements for cultivation. So the agriculturist must give the artisan and the weaver some portion of net product as remuneration. In other words industries should be there only to give fillip to agriculture.

However much we pride in industries you will not find common people—the masses celebrating the production of cars or ships. All over the globe harvest festivals are observed. This shows that the collective mind of the humanity is bent on farming and producing more food. Onam is a harvest festival. That is the natural order as posited by the physiocrats and this is revealed to every man through intuition, the light that lighteth every man that cometh to the world. Nowadays people are drawn to other occupations than farming. But the object of vocational education should be to reinforce agriculture. Once the food production is achieved, all students of vocational education are merry. That is what Dominic observes in "Harvest Feast."

> Those little people of Kozhikode,
> avidly feasting on rice and payasam;
> The harvest banquet of their sweated labour.
> . . . .

a lesson too to the adult world: ("Harvest Feast" 19)

No, Dominic does not praise the labourers at Bhaba Atomic Research Institute. In his red salute or "Lal Salaam to Labourers" the poet salutes the labourers who are backbone of the country:

> They sow the seed;
> reap the corn;
> and we eat and sleep.
>
> They spin and weave;
> make beautiful clothes;
> and we wear and 'shine.'
>
> They build houses
> where they never rest,
> and there we live and snore.
>
> They sweat in factories;
> produce numberless goods;
> and we use and enjoy. ("Lal salaam to Labourers" 28)

But it is a pity that these labourers are ill paid. Dominic observes:

> Let us not be stingy
> when we pay them wages,
> for we can't do what they do. ("Lal salaam to Labourers" 28)

And once again we must invoke the physiocrats on this issue. They assert that the equivalent of the annual expenses of the peasant and labourer should be borne. In this context the French philosopher Abbé Baudeau should be quoted elaborately:

> I say it boldly, cursed be every proprietor sovereign and emperor that puts all the burden upon the peasant and the land which gives all of us our sustenance... and that he who ennobles them furthers their comfort or leisure increases their output of wealth which after all the one source of wealth for every class in the society. (*A History of Economic Doctrines* by Charles Gide and others translated by R Richards George G Harrap, London, 1949, page 44)

Dominic exhorts:

> Give them at least their due;
> the more we give, the more we get;
> Put charity in humanity
> a spiritual bliss that never dies. ("Lal salaam to Labourers" 29)

This is the economics of charity in Dominic style. Which is more important, diamond or water? Dear economists, the utility of water is untold. But the utility of diamond is mainly for fashion parade. And since water and oxygen are in plenty and since diamond is scarce you decide the mining of diamonds as valuable production. How foolish you are! You do not know how much water and environment is being polluted. You do not know how to compute this degradation of the environment.

Dominic exclaims:

> Water, the source of life;
> Omnipresent and abundant
> like its parent oxygen.
> Free and 'insignificant'
> for millions;
> going to be more precious
> than gold and diamond. ("Water, Water, Everywhere . . .", 133)

Oxygen is the parent of water. This speaks of myth making power of Dominic that reminds of the myth making power of Shelley as evident in "The Cloud." In ancient Sanskrit and in ancient German the poet and prophet are one, vates or kavih. The way water is being polluted, in times to come water will be scarcer than diamonds. The economist and their mentors are idiots and the agents of ignorance representing the moon of ignorance hiding the Sun of wisdom. Samuel Taylor Coleridge in the context of a narrative depicting a sea voyage observes during a particular situation: "Water water everywhere but not a drop to drink." The earlier narrator forges a myth. But the later poet Dominic represents it as a symbol. Water is the source of life. Water or the compassion of God is everywhere. But we have been blinded by the elite of the society. Because of our ignorance we cannot derive our sustenance from the gift of Nature and we grow spectre thin on the edge of death in life. We have been blinded by the elite. They impart false education. They tell us that diamond is more valuable than water; the overhead is more valuable than the real commodity which has been produced. Consequently

> Education makes them crazy of
> White-collared cosy jobs
> Fertile arable lands and fields
> lie like deserted waste land ("Multicultural Kerala" 161)

This is not all. The land is being debased.

> Construction mania devours
> paddy fields and arable lands
> and defecate multi-storeyed structures
> on mother-earth's lovely bosom ("Multicultural Kerala" 161)

If you disfigure mother earth's lovely bosom with built space why should I not call it discharge of faeces of civilization? Think of the happenings at Singur in West

Bengal. Fertile land that gives crops thrice a year was given away to Tata the industrialist for manufacturing nano cars by the communist State government. Was it not sacrilege? Was it not disfiguring the mother's breast? Was it not selling away your mother for money by ungrateful children?

Chapter 3 - Pathos in the Poems

At the outset of our essays on Dominic we said that Dominic's poetry was engendered by pity just as Valmiki's. Ayodhya was a paragon of a city in the contemporary. The city was flanked between river Tamasa and Sarayu. While Sarayu comes from Lake Manasa, a lake made in the image of Brahma, the creator is charged with sattvaguna. Tamasa representing darkness was symbolic of Tamasika guna. While Valmiki was about to bathe in the Tamasa he was shocked by a loud cry reverberating in the skies. It was the cry of a female bird whose spouse was killed by the arrow of the hunter. My readers are apt to ask: Where is the bird killed by the hunter? Where is the bereaved she bird? Where is the hunter in Dominic's poems? Which is the arrow that killed the bird? Well land is the bird disfigured by greed and technology. Water is the wounded bird marred and defaced by dams. Let us now look at the human incarnations upon the heath.

Lance Naik B Sudheesh at Siachen army camp had planned to visit home on leave to have a first glimpse of his darling daughter. Four month old daughter Meenakshi is shown her father's frozen dead body. Meenakshi and her youthful mother are the she bird. Sudheesh is the he bird killed by the hunter. The laments of the surviving bird shook the skies and the earth and the poets Valmiki and Dominic.

> What a depressing sobbing sight for mass assembled!
> Tsunami of groans, laments, weeps and sighs!
>
> ("Tribute to Siachen Martyrs" 243)

Dominic describes the situation with telling power:

> Alas neither of them identifies each other!
>
> ("Tribute to Siachen Martyrs" 243)

Meenakshi is not old enough to know her dad. Lifeless eyes of Sudheesh cannot see his offspring. Dominic is a master of evoking pathos. To that end he often employs sensory details in dramatic situation. Do we not see the child of Joson before our eyes when Dominic addresses his dead friend Joson:

> When your youngest kid,
> not knowing what has happened,
> kissed your face often
> and plucked flowers

from your wreath;
tossed them to her sisters weeping and screaming
What a game He plays!

("In Memoriam George Joson" 1)

Dominic shows us more than he tells us.

On Tragic Lives of Children

Curiously enough the very bereaved child with which the *K. V. Dominic Essential Readings and Study Guide* opens recurs at the end of the book and that is how the book comes full circle. And does it not remind us of pity like a naked new born babe destined to stride in the blast?

Our country is as it were the deflowered garden of a selfish giant where children are killed, abused and sold. It is the country ruled by Herod and Kamsa where children undergo mayhem:

Forty thousand children
Abducted in India every year!
. . . .
India bears three lakh child beggars!
Forty four thousand children
fall into gangs' clutches every year!
How can man be cruel like this!

("Child Trafficking" 224)

This is an instance of logos where arguments are put forward to persuade. Dominic juxtaposes logos with pathos or appeal to the emotions and empathy of the readers.

A child beggar Anand looks at the little boys going to the school in uniform making a joyful noise. But, nay all the earth does not break forth into joyous songs. Anand remembers how like a vulture a car came. A bearded man with a black towel swooped upon him, hushed his cries for help and pushed him into the car. And now he is begging. Anand reflects:

Many months have passed
since I left my mummy, dad and Smitha
Are they still crying at my loss?

("Anand's Lot" 10)

Right at this moment:

"Bloody dog, why are you standing still?"
The bearded-man slapped helpless Anand.
. . . .
Crying, Anand stretched his hand
went begging shop after shop. (

"Anand's Lot" 10)

Dominic is as competent in telling as in showing. The predicament of Anand has been so vividly brought home to the readers that it seems to us that the same has been taken from a leaf from the poet's own childhood.

Anand's lot is a leap into the well of life in death. And now think of Mahi's fate:

> Mahi's fourth birthday
> clad in new gaudy dress
> celebrating with her friends
> playing near the house at 11pm
> fell into the hellish trap,
> a deserted uncapped bore well
> seventy feet deep ("Mahi's Fourth Birthday" 194)

The destiny of Mukesh is identical. He has fallen into the cavity of poverty unaware.

> Born to impoverished Dalit parents
> . . . .
> Mother bedridden with mouth cancer
> Father, the bread earner
> fell victim to acute asthma
> Little Mukesh their lone support
> Works in nearby estates
> . . . .
> When his classmates enjoy holidays
> his nimble feet and soft hands
> clash with rough tools and hard earth   ("Mukesh's Destiny" 192)

The little child cries for the breast milk of the mother ("Cry of my Child" 55). It is an examination hall. May be Professor Dominic is the invigilator there. A mother hard pressed by economic exigency is sitting for examination. The examination hall is sombre and silent. But the hall is loud with the cries of the child that the mother alone can hear. She does not know what to do. She feels the prick in her breast.

The creator Brahma blessed Valmiki and said that he would be able to perceive everything visible and invisible associated with Rama. Valmiki's quest was for an ideal man.

Similarly at the biddings of God the Father, the poet Dominic shows the world God's grand concert in:

> . . . matter and spirit
> animate and inanimate
> visible and invisible
> tangible and intangible
> audible and inaudible ("Multicultural Harmony" 149)

In short the world system is as it were the theme of the poetry of Dominic.

On Hardships and Tears of Youth

Let us return to the theme of children in Dominic x-raying the dysfunctions in the world system. A little earlier we were at an examination hall. Now let us visit a school:

> A boy in tears stand on the verandah;
> A punishment for not wearing his tie!
> In the humid weather of forty degree
> a slavish mimic, a legacy of West. ("A Nightmare" 6)

Why does Rahul stand outside the class in tears?

> Couldn't study
> yesterday's portion.
> Whose fault?
>
> Drunken father
> beat mother,
> beat Rahul;
> kicked away supper,
> none could sleep.
>
> Cruel father,
> Cruel teacher,
> Cruel world,
> Poor Rahul
> longs for love. ("Rahul's World" 39)

Elsewhere:

> The child is reluctant
> to go to school:
> teacher welcomes with cane ("Nature Weeps" 117)

This is the real cause for dropouts in the schools. Primary level dropouts in Nagaland is 19.4 percent, Manipur 18 percent, Mizoram 13 percent and so on according to Smriti Irani, erstwhile education minister (indiatoday.intoday.in/education/story/drop-outs-in-north-east-india/1/0660697.html). But this is a white lie. The number of dropouts in schools in India is staggering.

Not only women and children but young men and old suffer from severe wounds. Let us accompany Dominic to the liquor shop.

> Blind old man
> weak and bony
> leaning on staff
> holding lottery tickets ("Lottery Tickets Sellers" 193)

Now let us to go to the bus stand.

> Similar sight of a ticket seller
> a youth who has lost
> both his hands
> pleads for commuters' mercy
> in buses after buses
> with tickets and money
> hanging in two pockets ("Lottery Tickets Sellers" 193)

These are visuals made of words. They remind us of the scream by the expressionist painter Edward Munch. Edward Munch makes visual art audible. We can hear the scream. Dominic makes verbal art visible before the eyes. For oft when we lie and loll lonely on our cozy cot in fine and dandy mood these ugly sights flash upon our inward eye which are the curses of solitude.

Nothing tangible is ugly with Dominic's aesthetics. He beholds God's beauty in all forms. He finds manifestation of Him in the face of Poppy the cat. But man distinguishes between the beautiful and the ugly. A little girl asks:

> Ma, why didn't God create me a little more beautiful? ("Beauty" 12)

The mother in Dominic responds:

> Who told you dear that you are not beautiful? ("Beauty" 12)

And Dominic asks:

> When will "crow crow" be
> Pleasing as "koo-koo"?
> When will the Black be
> kindred to the White?
> When will the Black and the White
> dwell in the same house
> and dine from the same plate? ("Crow, the Black Beauty" 105)

This is reminiscent of William Blake and *Songs of Experience*.

Apartheid is unnatural and goes against the system of God. True that God has created difference between the snake and the dove.

The Rig Vedas imagine that at the beginning of the beginningless there was the cosmic Purusha with thousand heads, thousand hands, thousand legs. And he sacrificed himself. From his head the Brahmins sprang. From his hands the Kshatryas or the warriors sprang. From his thighs the Vaisyas sprang and from his feet the Sudras sprang. The Brahmins had innate aptitude to sacrifice themselves for the wellbeing of the world. The Kshatryas had the inclination to rescue man from physical assaults. The Vaisyas had innate leaning for exchange of wealth and the Sudras had innate inclination for service. True that nowadays servants assume Masters, the elephants dictate the Mahut. May be the Brahmins are no longer selfless or sattvika. May be the caste system implies station and duties. May be caste system has relevance even today. But does it necessarily mean that Prakash Jaadav aged thirty one riding a motorcycle should be attacked by a group of twelve. He is beaten and his nose is slashed.

> The reason for this diabolic act?
> "The Dalits have no right to ride motorbikes
> in presence of high caste men." ("Caste Lunatics" 169)

On Man's Selfishness and Vices

With Dominic nothing is hateful in God's creation. God says:

> Rhythm is there
> in your breath;
> your heartbeats;
> . . . .
>
> your chew
> and munch;
> . . . .
> and even
> your flatus. ("Write My Son, Write" 76)

No word is profane for Dominic. While

> Birds and animals play
> their assonant keys.
> Man alone strikes
> discordant notes.
> . . . .
> It's your pettiness,
> viewing things
> in different ways,
> thinking in opposites;
> good and bad,
> beautiful and ugly. ("Write My Son, Write" 76-77)

In the self-same way, the humanity is divided into haves and have-nots--man made categories.

> never in creator's dream.
> . . . .
> When millions die of hunger,
> thousands compete for delicacies.
> What justice is there for the minority
> to starve the majority to death? ("Haves and Have-nots" 20)

What is a country but her people? A country is not its building or its airports or dams. Our ailing country is visible through her wounded people.

Think of the flower vendor who sells flowers to deck marriage parties and banquet halls. But his own daughter remains unmarried because he cannot afford dowry to the prospective suitor. Love is not love when it is mingled with some other consideration than love. The flower vendor's dear wife is bedridden with cancer ("Flower Vendor" 226).

Chapter 4 - Criticism on Government's Claims and Promises

Indeed India is number one in the world. But in what aspect?

> Ninety seven percent of my countrymen
> have no access to clean drinking water.
> Yet the government claims
> the country is fast growing!
> True, growth is there
> in numbers of multi-millionaires
> who are even less than two-percent.   ("India Number One" 166)

Who denies the:

> Rocketing growth of India!
> Overtaking America,
> surpassing Europe,
> competing with China?   ("Rocketing Growth of India!" 121)

But:

> Statistics never fails.
> First in population growth;
> first in number of poor;
> top in ignorance and illiteracy;
> top in superstition and fundamentalism;
> very low standard of living.
> Rocketing growth of the rich;
> express growth of the poor;   ("Rocketing Growth of India!" 121)

On Family

Family is one of the legitimations of Dominic's poetry. In a developing country like India, family is as it were the greatest casualty. From every cottage wails and laments blow and tears flow unimpeded. Scanty light on the road brings about the car accident of Joson and his children and wife weep. A mortal cavity on the road kills Mahi a four years old and her parents scream. In a gaudy mansion an old man and his wife mourn for their children who are away. Our country cannot give gainful employment to her sons and daughters. Now let's look at the case of slums:

> Not far away were the slums of the city;
> three generations lived in each hut;
> grandpa, grandma, their sons and their wives,
> and their little kids sleep in a room! ("A Nightmare" 7)

Lakshmi cannot get married because she cannot afford the required dowry. She says:

> Father died when I was ten,
> mother bed-ridden with cancer;
> a thatched house in five cents;
> an elder sister married off;
> My meagre salary two thousand
> hardly meets our food and medicine. ("Laxmi's Plea" 30)

Look into Rahul's family:

> Drunken father
> beat mother,
> beat Rahul;
> kicked away supper,
> none could sleep. ("Rahul's World" 39)

What a birth we Indians have:

> Just returned
> from the furnace
> after the tarring work.
> . . . .
> Drunkard husband
> will come at night
> to resume beats and kicks.
>
> Dawn for doom
> Dusk to damn
> What a birth! ("What a Birth" 42)

Rejected by relatives, neighbours and society, Chellamma, widow, childless, weak and homeless, counts down minutes and waits. The alien Death will arrive in train. ("For the Glory of God" 108)

Lo there is a lady whose husband has eloped with a harlot leaving her three daughters. She has father and mother bedridden. She climbs a tall thorny tree to earn her bread. ("Resolution" 120)

Are not these shattered families the basic constituent of the society that is developing India? Teresa sweeps classrooms, veranda, campus. Her husband is bedridden, paralyzed by accident; two little daughters in primary school; life in a rented hut; debts to neighbours. She is in tears when she gets her one year salary because she must give it away to the manager. It is a forced donation ("Teresa's Tears" 124).

On the bureaucracy of India Dominic writes:

> In democratic government
> people are masters and
> bureaucrats servants
> . . . .
> Masters request servants
> "Sir, what shall I do for you?"
> It's our curse here
> bribes and graft rule service   ("Servants Assume Masters" 241)

So a country is neither tall buildings nor banquet halls but her people. And we have already surveyed the people of India through the eyes of Dominic. No better and truthful portrait of India could be gleaned anywhere in modern Indian English poetry. Their economy, their family, their housing, their economic activity that includes begging, have been depicted from firsthand experience. They are the wounded bird.

On Hunger and Poverty

Curiously enough India is a welfare state. Hunger led thousands to swarm at an Ashram and there was a stampede. Sixty three women and children died. Many were injured and hospitalized.

> PM announced ex gratia
> of two lakhs each for the dead;   ("Rocketing Growth of India!" 121)

Dominic's comments are being identified with the readers:

> Had the government granted
> half the amount when they were alive;
> had the government shown half the love
> they shower to the rich,   ("Rocketing Growth of India!" 122)

Let us visit a Tsunami camp led by Dominic:

> Months have passed
> since Tsunami tossed them from their houses.
> . . . .
> Government gave kits and boxes;
> kits don't contain essential things;
> hearth produces smoke than flames.
> None hears their cries and complains:
> "Where have gone the crores
> collected for their relief?"   ("Tsunami Camps" 17)

The government is indifferent to these helpless people that when these half fed, ill housed, deprived from clean water, men cried:

> "Give us boats and nets,
> and we will earn our livelihood."
> ....
> not even gods listen to their cries. ("Tsunami Camps" 17)

Now dear readers with your leave may we take the liberty to peep into the pompous state of affairs of the rich two percent of the country.

There is a mother who exhorts her child not to eat more than what he needs and must not waste his food. The mother says:

> Dear, you don't realize
> the price of your leavings;
> it can save
> a child like you
> from his death today. ("Hungry Mouths" 181)

The little child speaks in response:

> "Very very sorry Ma
> I will never waste
> any food in future.
> Ma, we shall keep
> a portion of our food
> and send it to
> those hungry mouths." ("Hungry Mouths" 181)

But such angels of a rich mother and a son are rare in our country.
Dominic tells us:

> I could view the cry of an obese boy
> whose mother was beating him to eat more.
> A cry of a different note was heard from the next door,
> where a bony child was crying for a crumb.
>
> A lavish wedding feast was served in the town hall,
> rich delicacies heaped on the plates,
> ....
> I could see two ragged girls outside,
> struggling with the dogs in the garbage bin. ("A Nightmare" 6)

The contrast of black and white brings both the colours pronounced. To use contrast and antithesis is one of the most effective devices of Dominic's poetry to reveal the difference between the rich two percent and the starving masses in clear terms.

The landless poor migrate to work on landowner's vast farm in exchange for paddy grains. No wages but one by twelfth of the harvest that too deducting the food they eat. This landowner belongs to the two percent affluent. 8th January 2013, the hired truck carrying sacks of grain they earned swerved and overturned.

Twenty five labourers and ten children died suffocated under heavy sacks. The grains for which they struggled hard--the grains in heavy sacks fell on them and led them to their graves. These are the ironies of life. No one, neither the landowner nor the government came to help their bereaved families ("Why is Fate So Cruel to the Poor?" 204).

On Fake Development

Perhaps development could rescue the masses grovelling in the dark in hunger and pain:

> Proposed Aranmula International Airport
> A dream project of private construction group
> Intends to construct airport city in 3000 acres
> Eighty percent land paddy fields and wet lands
> Rice and fish can earn four hundred crores per year
> Runway being constructed over tributary of Pamba
> Will lead to flood in river during monsoon
> Razing of four hills for filling wet lands
> Leading to water shortage and loss of biodiversity
> Will affect serenity and sanctity of Parthasarathy temple
> Three thousand poor families to be evicted
> But they are not willing to leave
> their sustaining lands, jobs and houses
> ("An Airport Made of Tears" 221)

The government and the corporate houses are in league to hasten development of our country at all costs. Let thousands be evicted from their homes. Let nature be maimed but development cannot stop. Who will benefit thereof? Why? The rich, two percent.

Truth is bitter and cruel. But Dominic is wedded to truth. The wings of the Pegasus of his poesy are cropped off. He makes us come out of our glass houses and carries us across the heath hewn into hell by the magic wands of development.

Urbanisation is sine qua non with development. Cities are the centres of economic activity. Money flows there with greater force than in villages. And surely the poor among the villagers throng into the golden cities of their imagination to conquer gold. And what happens?

> the city dwellers--
> Busy and selfish.
> devoid of humanity
> Each one lost
> in his own island.
> ("City Versus Village" 54)

Some neighbour is dead. The poet's wife asks the poet to go and seek. The dirge is however from a close house. Though nearby a hundred meters the poet and his wife never visited the house. The residents of the neighbouring house also never visited the poet. How can I go there? In contrast a village is an extended family where harmony and love rule. With the poet the villagers are fooled and cheated and looted by townsmen. In fact whatever surplus is created in the villages is invested in towns only.

During summer the poet lies in his concrete house fighting against the manmade heat and the dreary sound of the hot wave fan. On the other hand, cuckoo lies on his God given bed caressed by the gentle breeze, lulled by the nocturnal music. It has a sound and carefree sleep ("Sleepless Nights" 40). So this is how city life deprives man of the gifts of God.

So as civilization progresses, poetry declines. As development accelerates every man is caged and cabined, banished from the larger community of men.

The poet strikes a humorous note in his poem "Sail of Life." His morning walk takes him to a tea stall. He is really astonished by the din and bustle that comes out from all open stalls in the evening. The poet says:

> My boisterous sail will reach
> its harbour one day
> I will be astonished
> by its stillness and darkness.   ("Sail of Life" 187)

The humour here reminds one of Chaucer. Chaucer during his journey to the house of fame on the wings of an eagle through the blue deep pined for the muddy roads of London to which he was used.

Chapter 5 - Surrealism in the Poetry

On another level if stillness and darkness were the signifiers of death, then, is not a city where everyone is an island a metaphor of a hecatomb? True that when men are separated from each other cabin and caged, the dogs mingle with their kind and the crows often gather in spontaneous seminars where everybody has the right to caw. Thus development is the hunter, urbanization is the hunter, their child hunger is writ large on the faces of the majority of the Indians. But this is not all. In other countries also hunger walks like a demon. In Zimbabwe, the carcass of a wild elephant consumed in ninety minutes by avid famished men and women and children. The poet adds that even the skeleton was axed to support sinking life with soup ("Hunger's Call" 112). This grotesque scene of famished people eating up an elephant could constitute a surrealist drama in the developed countries. But what is surrealistic in the developed countries could be real in many parts of the world. The grotesque site of an elephant being eaten up by men lulls our conscious mind so that the message enters into our subconscious and redeems our beings. Thus Dominic is a surrealistic poet par excellence when occasion demands.

On Docupoetry

Mara in battle array accompanied by his friends and impish children, countless in number, attacked Lord Buddha when he was seated below the peepul tree determined to attain enlightenment. Humanity is in a similar predicament attacked by the forces of development, globalization, casteism, communalism, terrorism, hunger and many others in the trail. They could be characters in the Morality plays. They incarnate in the shape of real situations in the docupoetry of Dominic. Yes, just as plays composed by Hocchuth, Kipphardt and Peterweiss composed docudrama which has unswerving fidelity to history. Dominic's poetry should be called docupoetry because of its wonderful veracity as to the real shape of things in India and the world.

Now let us look at communalism as a hunter. There was a college teacher in Kerala, TJ who set a question paper in which certain questions were asked in the form of dialogue for marking punctuation. The quoted passage was in the approved and prescribed text book taught in the college. It hurt the sentiments of a few fanatics of a particular community. The fanatics set up its own court and in obedience to the dictates of the court, some miscreants of the community hacked off right palm of the professor. It was picked up by his sister and in the hospital stitched to like a dry branch budded to a live plant. They axed his left leg from thigh to toes. They cut three fingers and bones of left palm. Any reader can visualize the live figure of the maimed professor. It is more fearsome than Banquo's ghost. Neither Kyd nor Seneca could portray such figures. Facts are stranger than fiction. The image of TJ maimed and mutilated reminds us of the aesthetics of cruelty as propounded by Antonin Artaud. That benumbs our conscious mind and reason so that truth could be thrust into our being like a naked dagger.

But this is not all. TJ was suspended and dismissed by the college he served. Perhaps that is why Dominic exclaims:

> India, my independent country!
> . . . .
> Largest secular state!
> . . . .
> Where is freedom of speech
> and expression? ("To My Colleague" 126)

Dominic is not satisfied with the delineation of the assault on the professor. He describes the untold suffering of the professor. He was bedridden for forty three days

> Physical pains playing like concert;
> added by arrows darted by all sides: ("To My Colleague" 126)

Such a pulsating description of pain racking the body and the body suffering the same--a visual imagery and kinesthetic has never been put in words before.

On Violence, Terrorism and War

How about the world war-torn and jealousy-torn? Dominic exclaims:

> I wish I had the claws of a vulture
> to fetch the skeletons from Iraq
> and build a bone-palace
> to imprison Bush in it.
> . . . .
> I wish I were a bullet
> and shoot into the heart of the terrorist
> who compels the teen age boy
> to explode and kill that innocent mob. ("A Blissful Voyage" 5)

Just look at the grinning face of Dominic on the back cover of the book *Essential Readings and Study Guide*. It has the love and innocence of a child. Until and unless ye be like children ye cannot enter into the kingdom of heaven. Is such a tender face capable of such anger that it could become a bullet into the heart of a tyrant or a terrorist?

A train blast takes place. A hundred and fifty die. All innocents set out for nearby destination end at eternal terminus ("Train Blast" 128). Dominic informs us: "Another heinous act / of Maoists." They should be cursed as Ashwatthama was cursed. Ashwatthama killed the innocent children of the Pandavas. Just as God the Father cursed Cain, so was Ashwatthama cursed to live evermore and wander in the forest friendless homeless all alone. We have already named a few forces that are working to bring about misfortunes upon mankind and especially upon the sons of our dear mother India. Politics, religion are surely responsible for them but above all ignorance and economics initiating mankind with the mantras of development are the think tanks behind the architects of these misfortunes. It is their teachings that conjure war.

Well war is a judgment, says Dorothy L Sayers, that overtakes societies when they have been living upon ideas that conflict too violently with laws governing the universe... Never think that wars are irrational catastrophes; they happen when wrong ways of thinking and living bring about intolerable situations (Quoted from E. F. Schumacher, *Small is Beautiful*, Rupa and Co, Calcutta, 1974, page 30) Does not Sayers statement liken poetry? And does not Dominic speak like an economist when he the poet addresses us, man and posits:

> My dear fellow beings
> . . . .
> The entire system
> is a grand concert
> composed by the Solespirit
> . . . .
> visible and invisible
> tangible and intangible
> . . . .
> are instruments multitudinous
> of His perfect symphony.   ("Multicultural Harmony" 149)

Dominic elsewhere speaks in the parole of God the Father:

> None else shudder
> when I speak
> through thunder.   ("Write My Son, Write" 82)

Elsewhere:

> Lightning and thunder
> God's fireworks
> Frightened man quirks! ("Nature's Bounties" 33)

And yes, God sometimes speaks through thunder when the system of universe is jarred. What impels God the Father to speak through thunder? Karl Marx has been prophetic. He told that culture is the superstructure and economic forces constitute its substructure. We do not know whether the titanic economist Keynes said with sarcasm or not, but the fact remains that he counseled that economic progress could be only achieved if we employ those powerful drives of selfishness that goes against the tenets of religion. (Quoted from E F Schumacher, *Small is Beautiful*, Rupa and Co, Calcutta, 1974, page 24)

> Laws of Vasudhaiva Kutumbakam
> eternal laws of the planet
> Meant for humans and nonhumans
> But rational human beings never care ("Vasudhaiva Kutumbakam" 245)

Economists, the prophets of market economy sound the drum of competition that will have no ending. Systematic cultivation of greed and envy through the agency of politicians and religion and economics drive men to war. The drum that goads us to competition turns into war drums.

There is no participation of the common people in war. Dominic avows that man is not born with innate propensity for war.

> Aren't the masses peace lovers,
> benevolent and compassionate? ("Martyrs at the Borders" 198)

Love for the family, love for the village, love for the State where they inhabit, love for the nation/country are alright. But they do not support war between countries.

> More than two thousand soldiers
> sacrificed their precious lives for India and Pakistan
> While hundred and fifty crores of people
> cosily sleep with family in both the countries
> ("Tribute to Siachen Martyrs" 243)

No this is not indifference of the masses to the patriots of the country.

> People aren't iron-hearted to see their patriots
> suffer so sorely and sacrifice their precious lives
> ("Tribute to Siachen Martyrs" 243)

When wars are but fabricated by the whoppers of the politicians people are uncaring.

War drains away lot of human resource. Children lose their father. Wives lose their husbands. Parents lose their sons. Besides militarization of economy drains away the wealth of the country:

> When thousands die of hunger everyday on either side
> hundreds millions are spent on this vulnerable place
> ("Tribute to Siachen Martyrs" 243)

Dominic does not lament merely for the wastage of money in the country's defence. The demonstration of fire power at the desert of Pokhran – Vayushakti 2010 may have raised the approbation of the whole nation including President, Defence Minister and so on. Proud moments for all of them, but Dominic shudders at the sight:

> But for me a horrible sight.
> The dropping of each missile,
> an explosion in my heart.
> My mind can't conciliate
> though only a parade.
> . . . .
> One day or other
> my sisters and brothers
> in Pakistan and China
> will be burnt with such missiles.
>
> ("IAF Vayu Shakti 2010" 113)

Aristotle, as we have already observed, speaks of three kinds of persuasion in ethos, logos and pathos. And this is an instance of ethos.

War Dominic points out is a ploy of the politicians to divert the attention of the people and to muffle the protests of the masses against rampant corruption. And to that end they spend billions in defence.

> Total money spent on defence
> can wipe out poverty from the planet for ever
>
> ("Martyrs at the Borders" 198)

Military camp and war at Siachen, highest battle field in the world, is not war between two countries but war against nature. The avalanches there are mortally wounded. It is the selfish thoughts of a few people who devastate the system ("Siachen Tragedy" 156).

Mother India is the wounded bird as it were in her deathbed. Her own children, the crafty politicians, shoot mortal arrows at her. The poet addresses Mother India:

> Your politician sons suck your blood
> Rape you and even attempt matricide
> They shoot arrows and you lie bleeding
> . . . .
> you are dying inch by inch day after day
>
> ("Mother India, I Weep…" 235)

On the Need of Harmonious Life with Nature

Nature is also causality. It is the wounded bird. When Joson's little child plucked flowers from the wreath, it unconsciously signified that the beautiful things and tender things are not required where there is a travesty of civilization. In this green world made by man, a mallard becomes the mount of a poet. It is a pity that the present day civilization has brought to reality the state of nature as portrayed by Hobbes in Leviathan. In the face of the nascent jungle of civilization, man has to mutate into animals or else he will not survive. The poet develops the claws of a vulture ("A Blissful Voyage" 5). The poet mutates into a hawk ("A Nightmare" 6).

This is a queer world where somewhere the road overflows with black water streaming from a tap. At another place a waterless tap laughs at the queue of women with empty pitchers in their arms. This is how the civilization handles the resource of nature or the gifts of God ("A Nightmare" 6).

How do we treat nature? Rather has nature anything to tell us men? A sheep tells us:

> superior you boast
> but inferior you become
> to the microbes that kill you ("A Sheep's Wail" 8)

Indeed we cannot put up any resistance to the microorganisms, let antibiotics do whatever they can. We plunder the fur from the skin of the sheep. We loot her milk. And when she grows old we kill her to feast upon her flesh. The resources that are in the nature should be preserved and protected with great care. But the civilization is marred. It destroys its resources. The sheep posits that she is also created by God. Both man and sheep are equal in God's eyes. True that man can kill her, but once she goes to heaven she will plead against man before God. On the day of judgment man cannot appoint any Palkiwala to plead for him.

Nature is one of the richest resources wherefrom men cull imagery in his day to day conversation. When Anand was with his loving parents he would go school like a butterfly. But when the car came to lift up, it came like a vulture ("Anand's Lot" 10).

Nature is the finest book wherefrom one could glean the truths of life. Bodily beauty Dominic observes is only one among the beauties. It fades and decays as a flower does. The impermanence of earthly beauty is underlined ("Beauty" 12).3

> The dancing of the plant;
> the smiling of the flower;
> the chirping of the bird;
> . . . .
> herald Life's march here. ("Connubial Bliss" 13)

The cuckoo cries;

> "Wake up man and
> sweat for your bread"? ("Cuckoo Singing" 14)

If we could live in harmony with nature, our lives would have been as enjoyable as those of angels in heaven. But it is a pity that while the Cuckoo sings and loves, man exists sweating and moaning. When a man gets old and lonely, he likens a lily flower drooping ("Gayatri's Solitude" 15). Earlier children ran like butterflies and caressed plants and flowers ("Harvest Feast" 19).

Agriculture is the only art that gives man the joys of creativity. Nature is laid bare for man to derive its sustenance from her. The little children plough the land, sow the seed, pluck the weed, reap the corn, carry sheaves on their tender heads, thresh, husk, cook ("Harvest Feast" 19).

> Abundant Nature
> feeds plants and animals,
> Greedy selfish man disrupts
> Mother Nature's feeding;
> uproots millions of trees,
> exterminates thousands of animals.
> His deadly weapons
> pose great threat
> to life itself. ("Haves and Have-nots" 20)

Work Cited

Dominic, K. V. *K. V. Dominic Essential Readings and Study Guide: Poems about Social Justice, Womens' Rights and the Environment.* Edited by Victor R. Volkman. World Voices Series. Ann Arbor: Modern History Press, 2016. (The page numbers mentioned after quotes in this critical book is of this poetry collection)

Chapter 6 - Commentary on Selected Poems

Just as our mother, Mother India struggles for existence despite the attempts at matricide by the intellectual children of hers. Similarly Nature is also wounded just as T J was beaten by a band of fanatics, twelve of them. The sheep will lodge complaint against man on the Day of Judgement. The mango tree exists through his service to man and other creatures of God. He complains why man should cut him off. God the Father is Himself fed up with complaints against man.

Nature out of its love suo motu offers measureless resources for man to survive. Even the beautiful coconut tree gives us the model of architecture. The Dorian pillars were modelled after trees. If man lives in communion with Nature he will be happy. Happiness is heaven and heaven is happiness. Man does not realize this. He is destroying Nature. The temperature of the world is waxing. Thanks to globalization and toxic smoke in the air. Man axes the very branch on which he sits. He is committing suicide. A lady sans husband and children and rejected by the society went to railroad to commit suicide. But here is a fool who is amidst plenty and who is surrounded by his friend Nature who goes to death in an attitude driven by the delusion that he is the arbitrary ruler of all that he surveys. He is God as it were. But God is not an idiot like man. He is God because he is never arbitrary. He is all love and compassion.

Earth herself groans. Dominic hears her groans. A school of modern scientists now admit that the Earth is living. Consult the Gaia theory.

Now the question arises: how should we resist the suicidal attitude of man. Dominic does not believe in a bloody war between haves and have-nots. Dominic's poems constitute a picaresque novel where countless episodes figure. And it is a picturehouse of numerous selfless or sattvika workers. He believes in the efficacy of karma. And maybe he believes in the reincarnation of the soul. We must change the hearts of men with our sattvika karma. We must save our environment and Nature with sattvika karma.

On a particular plane he believes in Brahma, Vishnu and Mahesvara, the principles of creation, preservation and destruction that maintain the existence. But everywhere he sees the light that was never on sea or land. He speaks of Brahman who is neither involved in creation or preservation or destruction. He is the observer of his own activities or the activities of the trinity Brahma, Vishnu and Mahesvara. If this be true, if everywhere there is the master light, the light that was never on sea or land, that was ordained by God then we might pin our faith in Dominic who tells us that eternal beauty can be achieved. Om Shantih Shantih Shantih!

Explication of the poem "Siachen Tragedy"

> Siachen glacier
> milky white gray hair of Himalaya.
> Seventy kilometres long
> and height ranging from
> four thousand and six thousand metres
> Twinkling by sun, moon and stars
> Rarest beauty on earth for the heavens
> Winter, winter, winter, forever and ever
> Snowfall is thirty five feet
> temperature minus fifty Celsius
> Not a blade of grass grows
> yet world's highest battlefield!
> Thousands of soldiers of India and Pakistan
> fight with Nature to secure their frontiers
> Billions are spent for their outposts
> Siachen glacier feeding several rivers
> irrationally axed and dug
> Inviting vagaries of harmless Nature
> Avalanche lodged on seventh April
> buried hundred and twenty four soldiers
> and eleven civilians under eighty feet snow
> Isn't it high time the governments
> stopped challenging benevolent Nature?
> (*K. V. Dominic Essential Readings*, p. 156)

The poet's eyes move from earth to heaven and from heaven to earth and give locality and name to ethereal nothing. True, Xanadu is a place name like that. But to make Xanadu convincing Coleridge introduces Kubla Khan--In Xanadu did Kubla Khan...Well Kubla Khan is a name which we know and yet we do not know much about him. Kubla Khan stands for a twilight world where the wings of poesy can fly untrammelled. The name Siachen has a name and a location in the real world. And despite that we know it and yet we do not know it. It is also a twilight world fertile for poetry to flourish. In *Kubla Khan*, Coleridge gives us a vivid description of the course of the river Alph down to the sunless sea. Here the poet's imagination gives a name and location of a fictitious nothing that might stand for the course of life. But facts are stranger than fiction. Dominic gives us a vivid true to life description of Siachen heights that are as strange and romantic as the course of Alph made of fiction.

> Siachen glacier
> milky white gray hair of Himalaya

The Himalaya or the abode of snow is personified here true to the Indian tradition. Himalaya is a god. The poet Kālidāsa calls the Himalaya the king of mountains. And the venerable king of the mountains has gray hair. It speaks of the antiquity of the Himalaya and its wisdom. It is the ancient hill that, we surmise, Coleridge had in his mind in his phrase—forests as ancient as the hills. The poem "Siachen Tragedy" situates Siachen glacier on the head of Himalaya. Siachen Glacier is located in the eastern Karakoram range in the Himalaya Mountains. Think of Himalaya or the abode of snow. Vast snowscapes of mountains or mountainscapes of snow are so different from our landscape that our senses faint to describe them. They are what Kant calls sublime. They baffle our imagination just as the sunless sea in Coleridge baffles our imagination. The poet describes Siachen heights as ranging from four thousand to six thousand kilometres. And the glacier is seventy kilometres long. And since it is near heaven, twinkling by sun, moon and stars it is as it were a different plane of consciousness and a sight for gods to see. Yes it is a different plane of consciousness where winter, winter, winter, ever and ever where the madness fever and fret of our everyday world is frozen to inaction and tranquillity. Siachen means the land littered with rose plants. Siachen is the *sahasrara* of the Tellus as it were where thousand roses bloom. Coleridge did not give us the details of the upper course of the river Alph. May be Dominic, a professor of English unconsciously extrapolates the upper course of the river Alph through the depiction of the Siachen Glacier. Here

> Snowfall is thirty five feet
> temperature minus fifty Celsius
> Not a blade of grass grows

Is it not a savage place as holy and enchanted as ever beneath the sun and the moon and stars which was haunted by the laments of a woman for her god lover?

While Alph stands for movement and the phenomenon of change Siachen heights stand for perennial rest. While the river stands for ceaseless babbling the Siachen/Himalayan heights stand for perpetual silence. Siachen/Himalayan heights remind of the Mount Meru which is the centre of all physical, metaphysical and spiritual universes. It is the abode of demigods far beyond the sphere of man. But nay, nothing is static and at rest. Heraclitus comes to our mind--panta rei or everything changes. And with Heraclitus a mountain is a waterfall in slow motion. Look at the Siachen glacier, as if melted heaven slowly moves down the mountain to effect ablution of the earth.

But alas! Man today voyages to Mars and Moon. He climbs the mountain to reach the heavens. Earlier there was no human habitation in the Siachen Glacier region. But now army camps are situated at the Siachen heights and it is the highest battlefield in the world where thousands of soldiers of India and Pakistan fight with Nature. Here nature should be understood on two levels. When two men fight among themselves it is against human nature and Nature. The Indian and the Pakistani soldiers fight there to secure their frontiers.

At the same time they fight with the minus sixty degree Celsius to survive and they fight against Nature. Glacial ice is being cut and melted with chemicals. Bio degradable waste, use of arms, and ammunition have in no time turned a heaven upon earth into hell. Shocked at human behaviour, the glacier has been retreating. Is it not funny that billions of dollars are being spent to turn heaven into hell? Is that how science and civilization transform the gifts of Nature only to add to the sufferings of man? The savage place holy and enchanted that Coleridge knew is being defiled and desecrated and assaulted by man quarrelling with his fellowmen. It seems as if civilization knows no peace. If ever these civilized men reach heaven they will import war with their fellowmen there in the realm of time honoured peace and bliss. Ha Ha! Often laughter is but tears in disguise! We do not know whether Siachen tragedy fingers at the tragic predicament of Nature or the tragic predicament of man dying in cold or dying fighting each other or the tragic predicament of civilization. The poem is like the smile of Mona Lisa that baffles interpretation!

Text and Explication of the Poem "Massacre of Cats"

My next door neighbours,
husband and wife,
pious to the core,
go every morning
to church for Mass:
offerings to God.
Went this morning,
offering delicious
fish fry to all our
cute cats:
fish fry mixed with
highly virulent toxin.
Offerings at home;
offerings at church.
One after other,
all the four died,
struggling hysterically
for water and breath,
soft velvety fur
drenched in saliva
and excrement.
Heartbreaking carcasses
welled our eyes
and tears ran

like rivers.
With shaking hands,
dug a deep grave
and buried them.
The neighbours
celebrated the offer
peeping through
the window curtain.
How could they do this
demonic massacre?
They had complained,
the cats excreted
on their vast compound.
Cats always conceal
their excrement
with soil around.
Man has to learn a lot
from these humble beasts.
Where will
cats defecate?
Where will
all animals defecate?
Is this planet
man's sole property?
My materialist neighbours
go to church everyday;
read the Bible everyday;
but never read the part
to love other beings
as fellow beings.
Instead they believe,
other beings are
creations for their
service and taste.
God, instill in them
thy creation's purpose;
the need to love
other creations--
animals, plants
and the planet itself.
Kindly teach them
to learning to live
with the system.
Let my neighbours expiate,
dig out skeletons

> of my cats;
> tie them
> to their necks
> as Coleridge's
> ancient mariner
> did a century back
> since he killed
> the ominous albatross.
> God, open the eyes
> of all human beings
> and show them
> the flow of the universe
> and make them all
> as participatory beings.

(K. V. Dominic Essential Readings, pp. 94-96)

Dear Readers My head is today full of cats. I cannot get rid of them. Now you drive them away from the mind. And lo! You can hear them mewing or roaring and complaining from nowhere. Now you shut the call of the cats their carcasses flash upon the mind. Do you know who has put cats in my mind? The poet, K. V. Dominic. Ha! Ha! Dominic is a poet who writes about cats and cows.

Dear Readers may I take your leave most humbly to dwell on how Dominic has done the mischief of putting cats in my head? Dominic has composed a poem entitled Massacre of Cats. Ha! Ha! Is it not mock heroic? According to dictionary massacre means an indiscriminate and brutal slaughter of many people. The word massacre reminds us of the massacre at My Lai in South Vietnam where between 347 and 500 civilians were killed. Such real stories chill our blood and freeze. But think of massacre of cats. Unfortunate perhaps. But a little funny too.

But how did the massacre happen? May be some contagious disease infected them and killed them. But no. The poem begins with a pious family--the poet's neighbour. How lucky is the poet! Isn't it? To have a pious neighbour is a good fortune. At the very outset the poet evokes our reverence for his neighbours. They are a pious couple--a husband and a wife. When both husband and wife are pious there is a great flame of piety excelsioring. What do they do impelled by their piousness? The poet says that they go every morning to church for Mass offerings to God. The word Mass could mean different things to different people. But when it is associated with church it could mean entire church service in general.

With Catholics it is the source and summit of Christian life. Catholic Church believes that Mass is exactly the same sacrifice that Jesus offered on the cross. Why did Jesus offer his flesh and blood by way of being crucified? He did it to redeem every sentient being in the eyes of God, the Father. During every Mass in the Church the Eucharist is being enacted and re-enacted as it were verbally and through liturgy. The Miracle dramas of yore still persist. The experience at a Mass cannot be described in language. It is as it were an experience undergone during a swoon. The senses fail to describe it. And joining a Mass one also feels like a Bodhisattva whose only end in life is to serve the sentient beings and the so called inanimate things. And this Mass seems to be at the centre of the narrative embodied in Massacre of Cats. So the indicators of the husband and wife of our narrative as pious is proved by their regular attending of the Mass. This morning also they went to the Church but presently before going to the Church they offered delicious fish fry to all our cute cats. Mark the two lines-

> Offerings at home;
> offerings at church.

At the Church they will offer all their belongings to God the Father. At home they offer fish to the cats. "He prayeth best who loveth best all things great and small" (Coleridge). Once you love the slimy things angels appear and carry your boat across the ocean of suffering. But what happens to the cats? Are they not mewing out of great pleasure? That could be a possibility. But oh no. That possibility has been undone.

> One after other,
> all the four died,
> struggling hysterically
> for water and breath,
> soft velvety fur
> drenched in saliva
> and excrement.

Powerful word painting! We can see the cats dying. We are aware of their tender beauty. Our sense of touch is evoked by the velvety fur and lo! These beautiful creatures lie dead drenched in saliva and excretion. Those who have been killed in the wars or battlefields are seldom described in such telling imagery. Poetry here is in pity. The poet recalls how the heart breaking carcasses welled the eyes of the poet and his fellowmen. Tears ran like rivers. What was there in the offering of the fish fries? Poison was added to the fries. And what do they offer God in the Mass? When you find apparently pious persons proving themselves as murderous there is a sudden reversal of expected events—a peripeteia. And there is a story. A good man doing a good job does not make a story. But when we discover a good man to be cruel it is a story. The death of the cute cats reminds the readers the death of Duncan. "Oh horror! Horror! Duncan's silver skin laced with golden blood!" (*Macbeth*, Act II, Scene 3). And here soft velvety fur drenched in saliva and excrement.

The poet digs a deep grave with trembling hands and buries the four cats poisoned to death. The neighbours who killed the cats relish the scene peeping through the window curtain. Here only the narrative could end dwelling on how men are different from one another. While the poet weeps at the death of four cats his neighbours rejoice at it!!

Why did the neighbours poison the cats to death? The answer is simple. The cats excreted on their vast compound. Well, in other words the cats trespassed the compound of the neighbours. But the poet asks:

> Where will
> cats defecate?
> Where will
> all animals defecate?
> Is this planet
> man's sole property?

Trespass is an offence as decreed by Tort. Yes if the rats from my house go to yours you can bring charge against us in the light of Tort. But can man ever control the rats or discipline them? Besides man's right to property is ab initio bunk. Did man ever sit with dogs and cats and rats and snakes and get the right to landed property with their consent? Man is born upon earth just as dogs and rats are born. Everybody has the right to land. When man speaks of right to property he has robbed land from other creatures created by God. In the poem "Write My Son, Write" God the Father tells us:

> Birds and animals play
> their assonant keys.
> Man alone strikes
> discordant notes.   (*K. V. Dominic Essential Readings*, p. 76)

The neighbour poisoned four cats to death--a discordant note in the creation where harmony and assonance rule. One wonders why man should strike a discordant note! God the Father observes:

> Your selfish mind
> tries to ignore
> benefits rendered
> by these housemates.   (*K. V. Dominic Essential Readings*, pp. 77-78)

The cats are also housemates. And they help to keep rats and many diseases away. Also they keep snakes away. But this is not all. God the Father says:

> Your species
> can't live alone.
> Cattle, sheep,
> goats, donkeys
> dogs, cats
> swine, fowl
> I created
> for your company;   (*K. V. Dominic Essential Readings*, p. 78)

True. People who are at risk for depression, loneliness and isolation are relieved from their complaints if they befriend cats. The cats often bring to people sense of happiness and purpose who help them. Looking at the cats playing lowers the blood pressure. Thus we must realize what God the Father posits:

> Living beings and
> lifeless objects
> all inter-related. (*K. V. Dominic Essential Readings*, p. 77)

The poet observes in response to the complaints of the neighbours against cats:

> Cats always conceal
> their excrement
> with soil around.
> Man has to learn a lot
> from these humble beasts.   (*K. V. Dominic Essential Readings*, pp. 94-95)

God the Father also asks man:

> Why don't you
> learn from Nature?
> Animals and birds
> present you models.   (*K. V. Dominic Essential Readings*, p. 81)

The poet prays to God:

> Kindly teach them
> to learning to live
> with the system.
> Let my neighbours expiate,
> dig out skeletons
> of my cats;
> tie them
> to their necks
> as Coleridge's
> ancient mariner
> did a century back
> since he killed
> the ominous albatross. (*K. V. Dominic Essential Readings*, p. 95)

The poet often refers to the cats killed as my cats. This does not mean that the cats belonged to the poet's household. The poet has kinship with all things both great and small. Because he knows that every insect and animal has been created by God just as men are created by God. So all of us belong to one family. So the poet laments at the death of the cats as we do when our kin die.

The poet, as it were, in a rage says that the neighbours should dig out the skeletons of the cats and wear the skeletons around their necks. Indeed the fellow mariners made the ancient mariner wear the carcass of albatross in a huff. But the poet does not curse his neighbours by praying for decking them with the dead cats.

Soon after wearing the dead albatross the ancient mariner developed in him a love for slimy things. At once angels came to his rescue and he was redeemed.

God the Father addresses man and says:

> You are my own dear
> as mosquito is. (*K. V. Dominic Essential Readings*, p. 83)

God the Father further notes:

> It's your pettiness,
> viewing things
> in different ways,
> thinking in opposites;
> good and bad,
> beautiful and ugly. (*K. V. Dominic Essential Readings*, p. 77)

In fact God cannot create anything ugly. There is nothing ugly in the creation. And once ancient mariner learnt to love the slimy things he was redeemed. The poet wishes that the pious neighbours understand that the creation is a system where every so called trifle has its significant role to play and where everything is in harmony and everything is our kin. We must love everything beautiful or ugly because nothing is ugly in God's creation. This is how we can redeem ourselves in the eyes of God. And this is what we look forward to when we attend a Mass.

Thus the poem is a narrative apparently mock heroic in style, littered with surprise and woven with suspense. The object of Mass is at the heart of the poem. It is a revenge story the other way round. The poet wants his neighbours to be redeemed in the eyes of God. The poem is an interpretation of Coleridge's "Ancient Mariner" on another level. This is not all. The poem is an elegy with difference

Explication of the Poem
"Lines Composed from Thodupuzha River's Bridge"

> Looking down from your girdle bridge
> my eyes and mind bathe in thy morning beauty.
> Invigorating cool water gushing through your vein
> overflows my mind with eternal realities.
> Every second passed in our lives
> is irredeemably lost forever.
> Invisible Time flashes in meteoric speed;
> the waters I gaze now also flow beyond my eyes.
> Unlike the flash of bygone Time
> it is never lost but remains immortal.
> Born from the eternal Sahyas
> it merges into the eternal ocean.
> The Creator thus reveals To His creations
> His perpetual relation and incessant love.

Rivers and oceans are embodiments of cosmic reality.

(K. V. Dominic Essential Readings, p. 138)

Thodupuzha is a magic name springing from the unvoiced fricative 'th' with an 'o' or contracted vowel, navigating to 'd' another voiced consonant and a labial contracted vowel ending in the voiced fricative 'zh' with an expanded velar vowel 'aa'. Does not the sound of the name itself suggest the course of a river leaping forth from the green hills flowing down to the seas? 'Thodi' means a river. 'Puzha' means a river. In other words the name made of a compound word unites the opposites. And when we stand on its bridge we are as it were at the confluence of opposites where lot of energy is generated. The bridge is a girdle or a belt or cord defining the waist of 'Thodi-puzha' a damsel of a river. The poet stands on the bridge like a child clinging to the waist of its nurse or mother. The poet's eyes and mind are bathed in her morning beauty. Invigorating cool water gushes through the veins of the poet. And thoughts of eternal realities overflow the poet's mind. This is the state when man dips into the waters. At that time the awareness of the contingent vanishes and the realities show up. The flowing waters are certainly symbolic of the flow of time. Time that flows away is irredeemably lost. And despite that when one climbs the bridge between that which is and that which is not, one realises an eternity that cannot be expressed in words. The feeling of the same is being evoked by the poem. Hence it is a symbolist poem.

The river born of the eternal Sahyas merges into eternal ocean. The Sahya mountains hark back to Gondwana period of 150 million years ago. So they are eternal. The mountains are the abodes of gods. They are symbolic of eternally eloquent silence. From the eternally eloquent silence the river pours down into the eternally silent eloquence—the seas. The opposites are made of the same stuff. Life is a river that springs from eloquent silence. It gives a tongue to silence only to merge into the silence of eloquent seas. So life is a journey from eternity to eternity from silence to silence from eloquence to eloquence. And that which flows from eternity to eternity cannot be momentary. Hence the momentariness existence is a myth and Maya. The ceaseless flow or flux of existence is looked upon by the poet as ceaseless flow of God's compassion and love for the creation. And even though every moment of the prosaic past drops off and becomes the part of poetic and then vanishes like bubbles in the air, nothing is lost. This is what the poet realises standing on the bridge on the river of Time. The poem is laden with paradox. And in fact paradox of poetry! What cannot be communicated through prose must be told in poetry.

Explication of the Poem "Parental Duty"

What right have parents on their children?
What right has man on this universe?
Are we the cause of the existence?
This flow has started time immemorial

> Aren't we just bubbles of that great flow?
> You can't rein the flow of the system
> But simply flow like an autumn leaf
> Why then concern too much of your offspring?
> Never dig your grave as Dhritarashtra did
> Best is to be models to your children
> Leading lives of dharma and karma.
>
> <div align="right">(<i>K. V. Dominic Essential Readings</i>, p. 239)</div>

Nowadays the world is too much with us discussing rights. In our country it is assumed that parents do have at least certain rights on their children. The parents bring up their children. Consequently they expect that their children should look after them when they grow old and infirm. In other words parents may think that it is their legal right to be looked after in their old age by their children. The Welfare and Senior citizens Act (2007) makes a legal obligation for the heirs and children to provide maintenance to senior citizens and parents by monthly allowance. But is the right to monthly allowance from the children enough for the parent? When there is a divorce or separation, there is quarrel between the mother and the father of a child as to who should get the custody of the child. To get the right to possess, the custody of a child implies the right to fulfil the obligations to a child.

True, *right* might mean prerogative or privilege. But prerogative to serve a person or a thing, or in other words, prerogative to perform any duty could be a right. Thus right, a moral or legal entitlement to have or do something means slavery to something only by choice in this context. If philosophical accounts of parental rights and obligations are taken into account we feel that the rights and obligations associated with parenthood is neither grounded on biological consideration nor on natural relationship between parent and children. It is a social construct. It is a myth. And the parents claim that they have the right to decide for their children or the parents have the right to be looked after by the children. They are cherishing a myth in that case.

There are philosophers who think that children should have the same rights that the adults enjoy. If someone has better capacity in any particular field than any other person it does not mean that the lack of capacity of one will imply denial of one's rights. A difference in capabilities does not justify turning down the rights to children. From our point of view parents have been instrumental in bringing a child to the world. May be the inscrutable Nature willed the birth of the child. Parents may be instrumental in bringing up children. But the child belongs to the society and to the Nature. The parents have no right to possess the child. A poet may have been responsible for forging a poem. But once it is published it belongs to the readers. The poet himself might be one among the readers. Despite this we have a sense of possession over our children. This notion of ownership is psychological and based upon make-believe. It is distinct from legal ownership.

The notion of legal ownership is also a human construct. But since they are believed in by us and by our fellowmen who constitute the society, they seem to acquire a kind of objectivity. When two persons see a ghost it is deemed as objective. And our minds are full of such objective stuff and man is doomed to be a denizen of a world of make-believe. The poet thunders upon us: What right have the parents on their children? The next line of the poem is more scathing: What right has man on this universe?

The astronomers of yore thought that the earth was at the centre of the universe. With the advent of Copernicus the pride of place of the earth was shattered. Earth is just a planet like other planets and they all circum-ambulate the Sun instead of the Sun and the planets and the stars circum-ambulating the earth. With Newton and his successor astronomers and the advent of more and more powerful telescope the notion of our visible universe widened. It clearly pointed out that our solar system is just a solar system among myriads of such solar systems in the existence. The visible universe is at least 93 billion years across. None can see the edge of the universe. May be there is no edge of the universe. In the face of it our solar system itself is less than a midge and what is man there? So the universe does not care a crumb for man. All that man is concerned with is pleasure or pain. That is the sum or end of human life. But the universe is listless. Dumb forces are working there.

How come man could ever have *rights* on the universe? There is the searching question: Are we men the cause of the existence? Existence here has meaning on many levels. Existence implies all that exists. As we have observed earlier the multi-verse is measureless. All that exist are measureless. How could man whose presence here tends to almost nihility be the cause of the measureless multi-verse? Existence might mean the state of living or way of life. Our lives also are not in our hands. We were not born on our own. And we are never free to determine the course of our life. So the fact stands that we are not the cause of our existence.

With the poet the existence is a flow. True we cannot see the existence as it is. We cannot but look upon it through time and space. Everything whatever we espy in the world of eye and ear as well as in the world inward, changes every nano-second. Even our bodies and minds are ever in flux. Hence the existence as we perceive is but a sequence of phantasmogoric visions, a flow signifying the impact of time where nothing holds on even for a twinkle of an eye. The poet observes that this flow has started since time immemorial. Because empirically time has no beginning and in course of its ceaseless journey it lays bare ever new visions only to be withdrawn the next second to make room for other emergent visions. Here amidst this flow are we not mere bubbles that vanish into the thin air in a fraction of a second? Is it not funny that a bubble carried along a stream seeks to control the stream itself?

Once we understand our position in the multi-verse impelled by the arrow of time that never changes its course, once we know that ourselves being mere bubbles popping out of a flow, we can never ever rein the galloping pony of time. We should get rid of our foolish fantasies to control our children or baulk the existence. Earlier Newtonian physics thought that it could unlock the mystery of the universe. But right now in the light of chaos theory it is evident that Nature is unknown and unknowable. The existence is a very complicated system or network of myriads of forces impossible to decode. Hence instead of trying to baulk the arrow of time we had better float along with it. We cannot undo a flood or an earthquake. Our science can at best announce that certain areas are flood prone or earthquake prone. What we should do is to evacuate those areas.

But are we civilised enough to welcome our brethren come from earthquake prone lands? We must get rid of our obstinacies like racism, nationalism, religious fanaticism and the like to adjust with the freaks of Nature. Hence we had better float like autumn leaves along the stream of measureless existence which is ever in flux. To float like autumn leaves implies that we must not will anything in course of our life's journey. We need not be much concerned with our children or worldly affairs. The poet exhorts: "Never dig your grave as Dhritarashtra did." This is polysemic. Dhritarashtra a protagonist of the Mahabharata is a doting father who dug his own grave. How come? He was blinded with his affection for his children. He always supported the evil designs of his children to find them happy. The boundless cravings of his children for the right to things that do not belong to them brought about their own destruction. Nothing happened to Dhritarashtra personally. And despite that the poet says that Dhritarashtra dug his own grave. It is because of the fact that to find oneself amidst the graves of one's children is perhaps worse than to be in one's grave. And we must not dig our graves the way Dhritarashtra did.

On another level Dhrita rashtra means one who owns a state—the king. King Dhritarashtra of the Mahabharata is blind. Similarly the statesmen of our time are blind. The citizens of the state are their children as it were. Being too much concerned with his own children Dhritarashtra caused great damage to his children, his subjects and thereby dug his grave. The same takes place in India today. Just as the father should not always try to satisfy the cravings of their children, similarly the rulers must not dance to the tune of the caprices of their subjects. What could they do then? Well, the poet tells us that the fathers and kings must pursue the path of dharma and karma. Dharma or religion derived from religare is that which binds the world together. It speaks of harmony. Karma is that activity which is performed with a view to binding everyone together. In other words karma is the activity as prescribed by dharma. Once the father or king performs dharma and karma he becomes the role model. The children of the father or of the pater familias or a ruler are apt to follow their role model. If Dhritarashtra's activities meant digging his own grave, the karma or activities of a father or a king as prescribed by dharma will pave our way to eternal life. Hari OM!

Stylistic Analysis of the Poem "Long Live E. K. Nayanar"

Prof. K. V. Dominic claims in his preface to *Essential Readings and Study Guide* that since he gives priority to the content of his poems he does not pay attention to the style of his write up. That is why, he observes, his poems lack much imagery and other figures of speech. True. He is one among us, a common man sharing his emotions with his fellowmen--the common run of men. And his poems are deceptively simple. But are they really simple? Are they really sans rhetoric? Let us read the first seven lines of his poem "Long Live E. K. Nayanar":

> "Long live E. K. Nayanar"
> The mantra is being muttered
> by millions of your comrades.
> We are in a trance
> since you bade us "Good bye."
> It's impossible to believe
> our dearest CM is no more.
>
> ("Long Live E. K. Nayanar" 3)

There are some 48 words in the above lines and thirteen of them have either M or N distributed among the seven lines. Consequently there are alliterations. Besides, repetitions and variations make a pattern. So, sound system of the poem has a well wrought pattern. M and N are nasal sounds. They give you the sound of a bell. M is a stop consonant and nasal. So it gives us a note that leaves much in suggestion after being uttered. Another voiced soft consonant and stop consonant only repeating once in "Since you bade us Good bye" is a shift from the recurring sound of M and N and puts bell on a different key. Amidst the moaning sound generated by M and N the voiced sounds B and G of "bidding good bye" indicates a different parole. We can hear it as Nayanar bidding us good bye amidst the mourning of the masses. This clearly shows that Mr. Nayanar readily welcomes the journey to the realm from where borne no man returns. This is radio drama where we visualize a drama through hearing only. But the poet who is one with the masses exclaims that it is impossible to believe that Nayanar is no longer with us. This is how the poet casts his spell upon the readers. What is real is transformed into a dream. One wonders whether the death of Nayanar is a dream and not real. While our intellect and senses know that Nayanar has died, our hearts do not believe in what the senses including the intellect know. Dominic through his way of speaking or rhetoric awakens the heart of the readers against their senses. Thus Dominic is the poet who charges the hearts of the readers with feelings that revolt against the senses with subtle rhetoric. He is different. So Dominic's poems are not shorn of rhetoric.

About the Author

Dr. Ramesh Chandra Mukhopadhyaya, (b. 1947), MA (Triple), M Phil, PhD is a retired college teacher now residing at Belur Math, Howrah, West Bengal, India. A Bilingual writer (English and Bengali), he has been writing on different subjects for the last thirty years. He has his PhD in the Buddhist Philosophy. He seeks to retrieve the wealth of poetry when it is a revelation. Dr Mukhopadhyaya is a soldier of the Underground Poetry Movement in present day Bengali literature.

He has philosophically and critically interpreted K. V. Dominic's masterpiece poem "Write My Son, Write" and it was published as an e-book by Modern History Press in 2016. Dr Mukhopdhyaya has been awarded Ashutosh Mukherjee gold medal for writing a treatise on modern Bengali drama. He leads a group of online writers called Sefirah@googlegroup.com which has more than 150 members.

Index

A

A Blissful Voyage, 60
A Nightmare, 31, 32, 34, 48, 54, 56, 64
A Sheep's Wail, 29, 64
A Tribute to Sakuntala Devi, 15
Ammini, 25
Ammini's Lament, 24–25, 29–30
An Airport Made of Tears, 57
An Elegy on My Ma, vii, 4–6, 25–29, 41
An Ideal Festival, 14
Anand's Lot, 46, 64
Ancient Mariner, 76
Arundhatidarsananyaya, 22
Ayodhya, 11, 45

B

Barthes, R., 3, 19
Baudeau, A., 42
Beauty, 35, 49, 64
Bhaba Atomic Research Institute, 42
Blake, 2, 49
Brahma, 21, 45, 47, 67
Browning, 31

C

Caste Lunatics, 50
casteism, 59
Catholic, 4, 72
Chaucer, 58
Child Trafficking, 46
City Versus Village, 57
Coleridge, 43, 68–70, 72, 75
    Ancient Mariner, 76
Connubial Bliss, 33, 64

Copernicus, 79
Cromwell, 29
Crow, the Black Beauty, 49
Cuckoo Singing, 64

D

Devi, S., 20
Dhritarastra, 34
docupoetry, 59–60
Dominic
    defined, 4
dropouts, 48
Durgasaptasati, 27

E

elegies, 21–32

F

For the Glory of God, 14
Freud, 4

G

Galatians, 27
Gayatri's Solitude, 32–33, 64
George Joson, vii, 21, 22, 23
Gide, C., 41
GIEWEC, iii
Gondwana, 10, 77
guṇa, 7–8

H

Hardy, 19
Harvest Feast, 42, 64
Haves and Have-nots, 50, 65
Helen and her World, 35
Hindu Marriage Act, 5
Howard, E., 11
HUF, 5

Hunger's Call, 59
Hungry Mouths, 56

I

I can Hear the Groan of Mother Earth, 15
IAF Vayu Shakti 2010, 63
In Memoriam George Joson, 21, 20–24, 22, 45–46
India Number One, viii, 53
International Women's Day, 35–37

J

Joson, G., 20–24

K

Kālidāsa, 69
Karma, v, 7, 8, 80
Keats, 32, 35
Kerala, iii, v, viii, 10, 12–16, 21, 23, 59
Kubla Khan, 68

L

La Belle Dame Sans Merci, 35
Lal salaam to Labourers, 42
Laxmi's Plea, 37, 54
Lines Composed from Thodupuzha River's Bridge, 9–10, 76–77
Lines Composed Upon Westminster Bridge, 9
London, 9, 10, 11, 41, 42, 58
Long Live E. K. Nayanar, 12, 21, 23, 81
Lottery Tickets Sellers, 48–49

M

Macbeth, 73
Maha Bali, v
Mahabali, 3, 13, 15, 16
Mahesvara, 67
Mahi's Fourth Birthday, 47
Maoists, 61
Martyrs at the Borders, 62, 63
Massacre of Cats, viii, 31, 70–74
Maternal Attachment, 16
Maveli, 3, 13, 14
Milton, 29, 36
Miscault, 4
Mother India, I Weep, 63
Mother's Love, 26–27
Mukesh's Destiny, 47
Mukhopadhyaya, 35, 83
Multicultural Harmony, 39–40, 47, 61
Multicultural Kerala, 14, 43
Musings from an Infant's Face, 38

N

Nature Weeps, vii, 38, 48
Nature's Bounties, 61
Nayanar, E.K., 12, 15
Newton, 79

O

On Conservation, 21
Onam, v, 3, 12–14, 16, 41

P

Palkiwala, 64
Parasurama, 10
Parental Duty, 34, 77–80
Parents Deserted, 33
peripeteia, 73
physiocrats, 6, 41, 42
Plato, vi, 7, 20
poetryscapes, 2
Purusha, 49

R

Rahul's World, vii, 48, 54
rajasika, 9
Ramkrisna Kathamrita, 7
Resolution, 39, 40, 54
Rocketing Growth of India!, viii, 53, 55

S

sahasrara, 69
Sahya, 77
Sahyadri, 10
Sail of Life, 58
Saint Thomas, 7
Sankaracharya, 4
sattvika, 1, 7, 9, 49, 67
Sayers, D., 61
Schumacher, E.F., 61
Servants Assume Masters, 55
Shakespeare, 1, 6, 23, 24, 25, 39
Siachen Tragedy, viii, 31, 68–70
Sleepless Nights, 58

T

tamasika, 9
Teresa's Tears, 55
The Little Black Boy, v, 2
Thodupuzha, 9–12
Thodupuzha Municipal Park, 20
To My Colleague, 60
To My Deceased Cats, 31
Train Blast, 60
Tribute to Siachen Martyrs, 45, 62
Trump, 6
truth, 57
Tsunami Camps, 55, 56

V

Vaisyas, 49
Valmiki, vii, 20–21, 20, 21, 45, 47
Vasudhaiva Kutumbakam, 62
vermilion, 40
Victory to thee Mother India, vi, 16
Vishnu, 10, 13, 15, 67

W

Water, Water, Everywhere, 43
Welfare and Senior citizens Act, 78
West Bengal, 14, 44, 83
What a Birth, 54
What is Karma?, 7
Where shall I Flee from This Fretful Land, 16
Wolfgang, 15
Wordsworth, vi, 9, 10, 11
Write My Son, Write, 50, 61

X

Xanadu, 68

Y

Yeats, 32

Z

Zimbabwe, 59

Write My Son, Write
Text and Interpretation
An Exercise in Close Reading

Dr. Ramesh Chandra Mukhopadhyaya

"Write My Son, Write" is K. V. Dominic's longest poem, in 21 sections taken from his collection of poems entitled Write Son, Write. Dominic unabashedly tackles everyday issues of India such as the social injustice of poverty, man's crass exploitation of natural resources that ought to belong to everyone, terrorism, and the eternal beauty of the natural world. This poem is the manifesto of Dominic's views and philosophies.

About this work, K.V. Dominic writes, "People today are crazy after materialism, and divinity in them is being lost to such an extent that they give no importance to principles, values, family and social relations, cohabitance with human beings and other beings. Instead they are trying their maximum to exploit their fellow beings, other beings and the planet itself. If it goes like this, the total destruction is not far away. It is the duty of the religious leaders, political leaders and the intelligentsia to inject the lost values to the masses and thus preserve this planet and the inhabitants from the imminent devastation. Instead, majority of these leaders become mafias and inject communal and corruptive venom to the minds of the masses. Corruption has become the hallmark of these leaders and influenced by them the masses also deviate from the right track to the evil track. And who will save this society? Writers, particularly poets who are like prophets."

Dr. Ramesh Chandra Mukhopadhyaya's commentary provides the most complete critical analysis of the poem, section-by-section and line-by-line. Born in 1947 Ramesh Chandra Mukhopadhyaya M A (Triple) MPhil, PhD is a retired college teacher now residing at Howrah, West Bengal, India, A Bilingual writer (English and Bengali), he has been writing on different subjects for the last thirty years. He seeks to retrieve the wealth of poetry when it is a revelation. Dr. Mukhopadhyaya regards K. V. Dominic as a poet of a seer.

K. V. Dominic's Write My Son, Write--Text and Interpretation:
An Exercise in Close Reading (ISBN 978-1-61599-305-5)

From the World Voices Series

Modern History Press

K. V. Dominic Essential Readings gathers for the first time the three most important works of poetry from this shining new light of contemporary Indian verse in English: *Winged Reason*, *Write Son, Write* and *Multicultural Symphony*. A fourth collection of 22 previously unpublished poems round out a complete look at the first 12 years of Dominic's prolific and profound verse. Each poem includes unique Study Guide questions suitable for South Asian studies curricula.

Written in free verse, each of his poems makes the reader contemplate on intellectual, philosophical, spiritual, political, and social issues of the present world. Themes range from multiculturalism, environmental issues, social mafia, caste-ism, exploitation of women and children, poverty, and corruption to purely introspective matters. From the observation of neighbourhood life to international events, and everyday forgotten tragedies of India, nothing escapes the grasp of Dominic's keen sense of the fragility of life and morality in the modern world.

Praise for the verse of K. V. Dominic

"K. V. Dominic is one of the most vibrant Indian English poets whose intense passion for the burning social and national ailments makes him a disciple of Ezekielean School of poetry. His poetic passion for the natural beauty keeps him besides the Romanticists."

—Dr. A. K. Choudhary, English poet, critic and editor, Professor of English, Assam, India

"K. V. Dominic is a poet of the suffering masses and oppressed sections of the society. He tries to dissect corruption at all levels, political or religious, social or academic and presents it in its true colours with all the ugliness and monstrous greed."

—Prof. T. V. Reddy, reputed English poet, writer and critic, Emeritus Professor of English from Andhra Pradesh, India

K.V. Dominic Essential Readings: Poems about Social Justice, Women's Rights, and the Environment (ISBN 978-1-61599-302-4)

From the World Voices Series

Modern History Press

Inside one of Contemporary India's most Influential Poets

The twenty-four papers in *Philosophical Musings for a Meaningful Life* study the poetry collections *Winged Reason* (2010), *Write Son, Write* (2011), and *Multicultural Symphony* (2014), of Dr. K.V. Dominic and reveal his humanistic values and concept of universal brotherhood, his social criticism devoid of absurdity and obscurity, his profound concern for the marginalized sections of society, and his reverence for Nature. All the papers focus on the poet's anguish at the evils and the inhuman attitude prevalent in the society and necessitate harmony of existence. In the context of Indian English poetry, the papers find Dominic to be unique in his use of simple and plain language to address the vast canvass of human life and the neglected segment of human society. Further, the papers bring out how the universal appeal of Dominic lies in his ability to view the world as a sanctuary and acknowledge him as the promising voice of the present century for his belief in the interrelatedness of all lives that ascertains positive change in the individuals.

Dr. S. Kumaran, Editor, is working as an Assistant Professor in the Postgraduate & Research Department of English, Thiruvalluvar Government Arts College, Rasipuram. He is Associate Editor of two refereed international biannual journals, *Writers Editors Critics* (WEC) and *International Journal on Multicultural Literature* (IJML); and a Member of the Editorial Boards of various journals from India and abroad.

"This critical study on the poetry of Dr. K.V. Dominic deserves to be read closely for evaluation and to be on the shelf of every notable library. *Philosophical Musings for a Meaningful Life* will inspire scholars from the West to find rubies and diamonds in the Indian poetry of today."

—Dr. Stephen Gill, Poet Laureate of Ansted University

"K.V. Dominic's social consciousness is his chief forte. Not for a moment does he divert attention from the simple and innocent activities of ordinary human beings. From his lyrics originate feelings of eternal sympathy, peace, and fraternal unity."

—P.C.K. Prem, critic from Himachal Pradesh, India

Philosophical Musings for Meaningful Life:
An Analysis of K.V. Dominic's Poems (ISBN 978-1-61599-266-9)

www.ingramcontent.com/pod-product-compliance
Lightning Source LLC
Chambersburg PA
CBHW081841170426
43199CB00017B/2810